More Praise for *Roméo Dallaire's*

Waiting for First Light

National Bestseller
Longlisted for the RBC Taylor Prize for Literary Non-Fiction
Longlisted for CBC Canada Reads
A *National Post* Best Book of the Year
A CBC Best Book of the Year
An Indigo Heather's Pick for Non-Fiction

"An important look at the plight of returning soldiers. . . .
Dallaire's work adds to a growing understanding of the special
challenges and traumas faced by peacekeepers. . . . While the
average person might not be inclined to read clinical literature,
Dallaire offers something more: an honest, firsthand account—
and from a general, no less." —*National Post*

"The courage and intensity of [his] revelations are deeply personal and unsettling. . . . But there is much here . . . to inspire
and nurture hope. . . . Dallaire's book is an eloquent cautionary
tale about what can happen if PTSD goes unaddressed for too
long. . . . This is a valuable and rare look into the soul of one who
suffers from PTSD. On this merit alone it will stand as an important read." —*The Globe and Mail*

"Brutally revealing. . . . Dallaire's raw and emotionally devastating
new book lays bare his own inner torment. . . . If PTSD has had a
face in Canada over the last twenty years, it is Roméo Dallaire's.
His life story, in effect, is a personal history of how Canada, and
the modern world in general, has responded to PTSD." —*Maclean's*

"I was left reeling by this book, overcome by shock, dismay, amazement. I've never read anything about post-traumatic stress quite so stark, honest and graphic. Roméo Dallaire bares his soul to the world . . . it's an act of stunning courage and a literary tour de force."
— Stephen Lewis

"A stirring account from a tragic mission that crystallizes the necessity of ensuring invisible injuries are treated with the requisite resources, attention and time as those that are physical in nature. Bravo Zulu, General Dallaire. Canada, and the international community, thanks you for your leadership."
— Scott Maxwell, Executive Director,
Wounded Warriors Canada

"Roméo Dallaire's PTSD, stemming from his experiences and peacekeeping responsibilities during the horrific Rwandan genocide, has affected all aspects of his life for the past twenty years. With brutal honesty and characteristically unsparing of himself, he shows the reader how PTSD has caused unshakable guilt, perennial insomnia, persistent distress, complicated family difficulties and spiritual angst. Although this book is about pain, it is not about despair. It is a triumph. . . . This book is a compelling, evocative, educational and riveting inspiration to all of us."
— Matthew J. Friedman MD, PhD, Senior Adviser (and former Executive Director), National Center for PTSD, U.S. Department of Veterans Affairs, Professor of Psychiatry and Pharmacology/ Toxicology, Geisel School of Medicine at Dartmouth

ROMÉO DALLAIRE

with Jessica Dee Humphreys

Waiting for First Light

My Ongoing Battle with PTSD

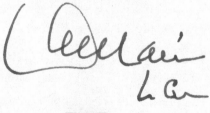

VINTAGE CANADA

VINTAGE CANADA EDITION, 2019

Copyright © 2016 Roméo A. Dallaire, LGen (ret) Inc.

Published by Vintage Canada, a division of Penguin Random House Canada Limited, in 2019. Originally published in hardcover by Random House Canada, a division of Penguin Random House Canada Limited, in 2016. Distributed in Canada by Penguin Random House Canada Limited, Toronto.

Vintage Canada with colophon is a registered trademark.

www.penguinrandomhouse.ca

Library and Archives Canada Cataloguing in Publication

Dallaire, Roméo A., author
Waiting for first light : my ongoing battle with PTSD / Romeo Dallaire.

Issued in print and electronic formats.

ISBN 978-0-345-81444-9
eBook ISBN 978-0-345-81445-6

1. Dallaire, Roméo A. 2. Dallaire, Roméo A.—Mental health.
3. Post-traumatic stress disorder—Patients—Canada—Biography.
I. Title.

RC552.P67D35 2018   616.85'210092   C2016-903978-1

Cover design: Five Seventeen
Cover image: © Guenter Guni / Getty Images

Printed and bound in the United States of America

2 4 6 8 9 7 5 3 1

Penguin
Random House
VINTAGE CANADA

For Willem, Flower and Guy,
and the generations to follow.
And for my wife, Beth.

Forthwith this frame of mine was wrenched
With a woeful agony,
Which forced me to begin my tale;
And then it left me free.

Since then, at an uncertain hour,
That agony returns:
And till my ghastly tale is told,
This heart within me burns.

—SAMUEL TAYLOR COLERIDGE,
   THE RIME OF THE ANCIENT MARINER

CONTENTS

Waiting for First Light

Esteemed General,
After reading your memoir of the holocaust that engulfed you
in Rwanda in 1994, it is striking that your anguish was so
akin to that of S. T. Coleridge's Ancient Mariner. . . . *After*
your premonition went unheeded, you were virtually aban-
doned by all but for a small band of brave soldiers. Thus you
were left powerless to halt the horror of the slaughter of
innocents by the génocidaires and, like the Mariner, as a
commander you felt steeped in guilt. Also like the Mariner
you endure the anguish of life-in-death. But you ultimately
mustered the courage and resilience to subdue it, then devoted
yourself to providing succour to the victims of war. . . . I offer
you the poem as a token of my respect and admiration. —IR

A FEW YEARS AGO, I received a package in the mail from the deputy head of UN Peacekeeping Operations during the Rwandan genocide, Iqbal Riza. An unfailingly sensitive gentleman, Mr. Riza had sent me a large, illustrated edition of Coleridge's *Rime of the Ancient Mariner.*

As I turned the pages, I became immersed in the Ancient Mariner's retelling of his doomed mission. I was struck by so many similarities between his story and my own: the burden of his command, his witness of unadulterated horror, his impotence, his guilt, his resolve. And his unconscious imperative, that maddening drive to educate the world about what he had experienced.

To summarize the story (in case high-school English class was as long ago for you as it is for me): an old man pulls a wedding guest away from the nuptial festivities and forces him to listen to his story. The old man had commanded a crew on a voyage of exploration, aboard a ship bound for parts unknown. When the weather turned rough, the ship was lost, and of all the crew, only their helpless captain survived. "*Water, water, everywhere/Nor any drop to drink*." The Ancient Mariner remained forever tormented by guilt: guilt at being alive when so many others died; guilt at failing in his command, failing to keep the others safe, failing his mission; guilt over his part in the tragedy, for which he is forever blamed.

The horrifying deaths he witnessed were senseless, and void of meaning, as was his remaining alive—a roll of the dice. But it is human nature to seek understanding through cause and effect, and so the Mariner relives again and again the moments before the horror, trying to understand what he could have done to prevent it. Rightly or wrongly, he blames himself for bringing on the horror by shooting an albatross.

The Mariner is burdened by both guilt and responsibility. The guilt—represented by the albatross hung around his neck—is relieved, at least a little, when he rediscovers beauty in place of his revulsion. However, his responsibility—imposed on him by a character called "Life-in-Death"—never leaves him: the eternal responsibility to tell the tale, since he was the commander, and the survivor.

I, too, was a commander who set out on what I thought was an exciting adventure, only to bear witness to the most terrible horrors on earth. I, too, was responsible for the mission, and therefore bear the responsibilities for the deaths. I, too, face blame—from others and from myself—for not preventing the atrocities. I, too, live Life-in-Death.

We—the Ancient Mariner and I—both became mired in guilt, both wanted so much to die but could not, and both eventually chose to take meaningful action. We persevere in our resolve to ensure the story is never forgotten, and that those who died did not do so in vain.

When each of us told our story in its entirety for the first time, we began a cycle that will continue throughout our lives: reliving the pain by telling the story, an action that attenuates the pain, which then returns upon the telling and must be relived to be relieved.

Teaching others by sharing our stories relieves us, temporarily, of our suffering. Of course, full recovery from a trauma this great is impossible and lasting serenity will forever evade us. The Mariner and I lived, when so many beautiful, innocent people died. The pain of that will never cease, and so we both devote our lives to sharing the story with others who might understand and learn. In this way, we attempt to build an ethical legacy, creating sadder but wiser humans.

I have already told my story of the Rwandan genocide. In *Shake Hands with the Devil: The Failure of Humanity in Rwanda*, and in speeches and presentations before and since that book was published, I explained what I saw. What I did. What I was unable to do. While I have not been silent about the injury I sustained in Rwanda, I have kept mostly private the effects of that injury on my mind, my body, my soul. Until now.

In this book, I describe how I came to live with an operational brain injury called post-traumatic stress disorder: PTSD. It is not an instructional manual on how to get better or an inspirational text of my triumph over adversity. After more than twenty years, I'm not "better," any more than a soldier whose leg was blown off is able to grow a new one. But as that soldier can adjust to this new reality—physically with prosthetics, crutches, a wheelchair; emotionally with professional, personal and peer support—so, too, have I learned how to cope, with some small victories and plenty of defeats.

Due to the nature of my injury—the resultant sleep deprivation, flashbacks, nightmares and emotional turmoil, plus the medications I must take to mitigate even worse effects and the manic pace of work I've undertaken as another way to cope—my memory has necessarily suffered. I cannot guarantee the absolute accuracy of every detail shared in this book. What I do promise is that these pages tell the true story of how I've felt and how I have perceived the world around me over the past twenty years, living under the pervasive and ever-present shadow of PTSD.

My sharing this story will have been worth it if, as a result of reading about my experience, even one soldier, one parent, one spouse, one child may better understand the effects of this long-taboo and long-misunderstood operational injury.

PTSD, which was known in the past as "shellshock," "battle fatigue," "combat stress reaction," and even derogatory names such as "malingering," destroyed the person I was. That carefree, vital man became two men in the wake of the injury. One is the person you meet, still duty-bound, whose emotions are identifiable and whose reactions usually seem normal. The other is the man inside me, the one who never really came back, who still lives on the battlefield.

This duality causes an eternal crisis that I unceasingly try to navigate. That inner person is the one that drives the outer man to act (in both senses: controlling his behaviour, as well as causing him to feel like an imposter of a human being). But that inner man is often impossible to control, and overwhelms the outer one, even tempting him with suicide.

The last time I experienced that temptation, I emptied the better part of a forty of Scotch. I found my father's old army shaving kit—the blade must have been five decades old. I was sitting in the living room, toying with it, and I just started cutting.

Not deep, just enough for the blood to flow. The warmth of the blood was so incredibly soothing. It didn't hurt; it was a complete release. I did my legs, my arms. The blood was flowing.

That's when they found me.

CHAPTER ONE

The many men, so beautiful!
And they all dead did lie:
And a thousand thousand slimy things
Lived on; and so did I.

A PAIN SHOT THROUGH MY arm, from the shoulder right
down to my fingertips, waking me. I struggled upright,
and squinted through the darkness, seeking the source. A
sniper's bullet? A grenade? Years of artillery training and months
of war had made me immune to the sound of explosions, so it was
entirely possible that I'd missed it.

Confused, I tried to attune my senses to the unfamiliar darkness and the curious silence. I was clearly indoors, but this was not
my office at the Amahoro Stadium in Kigali. Since the war began,
I had slept at my desk, with lights blazing, ready to take immediate action. Three, four hours, tops. The sounds of the deep
night—animals rustling, babies crying, the fax machine whirring,
the crackle of the walkie-talkie anticipating a call for help from a
vulnerable field post, distant (and often not so distant) firefights—
these had been the faithful companions of my sleep.

In contrast, the silence of this room was a solid mass of noise-lessness, unnerving after the din of the past year. Over the months of the genocide, the ceaseless cacophony of birdsong and bullets, of cries and commands, was only muted in death: whenever we came upon a village after a massacre, even the birds were silent. The quiet was absolutely deafening. We would gently pick through the bodies, searching in vain for survivors, pausing some-times to lower a raised and bloodied skirt, or turn a tiny broken body toward its still mother. The heavy scent of burning mud huts and coagulating blood hung in the air, but it was the smoth-ering silence of death that was so definitive, so absolute, like nothing else. Then a passing bird would begin to sing again and that sound would change the texture of the moment, relieving us from that insufferable, suffocating silence.

The pain fired through my arm again. I winced and tried to reach out for a light, but my arm wouldn't cooperate. I lay back, the feel of the smooth sheets and the soft mattress alien to me. Finally, a smell reached my nostrils—fetid, but familiar, and therefore comforting; it was coming from my boots, on the floor beside the bed, still wet and caked with mud. The mud of Rwanda.

Recognition washed over me. It was the morning of August 20, 1994. My request to be relieved of duty had been granted. I was in a hotel room in Nairobi, five hundred miles from Kigali. I had just come out of hell.

The events of the past twenty-four hours rushed into my mind, casting out the possibility of sleep.

Rwanda, August 1994

Yeah, the girls are out to bingo,
and the boys are gettin' stinko,

and we'll think no more of Inco,
on a Sudbury Saturday night.

The tinny sound of a Stompin' Tom cassette mingles
with bursts of laughter and the clink of beer bottles.
We do not speak of the events of the past year, but the
emotions we have been holding inside—the agony, the
rage, and the bond that only brothers in arms know—
come out tonight in hilarity and in tears, as my troops
bid me, their force commander, farewell.

Over the past few weeks, with the genocide essentially
over and the international community arriving in waves,
we had all begun to allow ourselves to suffer. It was as if,
now that we had made it through, everything we had
employed to hold ourselves together was snapping loose.
The cavalry had finally come—too late for the eight
hundred thousand human beings, children, women and
men, who had been brutally slaughtered in their homes,
schools, churches and villages. But they have come.

Only the rescue isn't working as we had hoped it
would; it is more like a cruel mirage.

A shipment of water-carrying trucks arrives from the
United States. I have twelve thousand parched and
starving Rwandans in this stadium alone. We have all
gone for days without any clean water to drink, after
weeks of tight rationing; babies are already dying of

thirst, their dehydrating mothers no longer able to produce breast milk. We had been unable to find a water source inside the country—the rivers and wells are poisoned by putrid corpses—so I had called the UN chief administrative officer, myself, to request a shipment of potable water. He told me that before he could send us a shipment he had to conduct a call for proposals and do an analysis of the three best bids.

Yet now, we are saved, and we are elated—until we learn that the trucks are intended for the refugee camps in Goma. The plane had landed in Kigali by mistake. It would have been funny, in a darkly humorous way, except that it wasn't. We watch the source of life for thousands fly off without even a glance back at the suffering they are leaving behind.

My staff is visibly tiring. Several are blank and unresponsive. Others are irritable and emotional, sickened by people posing for photo ops by mass graves and stepping over bodies—outsiders who hadn't been with us when we needed them the most. Hundreds upon hundreds arrive, and instead of reinforcing us they push us aside.

My daily lists are a hundred items long. I'm losing my temper, becoming unrealistically demanding. My manners and sense of humour—both essential to good leadership—are fading fast.

Refugees returning home to Rwanda are being inter-cepted by the Interahamwe, attacked, mutilated, and sent back to refugee camps in Zaire* as examples. The United Nations High Commissioner for Refugees (UNHCR) isn't helping to repatriate people because of the lack of protection available inside Rwanda; as well, the agency is concerned about returnees spreading cholera from the camps. The *génocidaires*—the people who wielded the machetes during weeks of slaughter—are running the refugee camps and re-arming.

The NGO community is trickling back, as is my UN mission staff, and there is a steady influx of dignitar-ies and diplomats. They all seem shocked at finding the place in such disarray—orphan kids everywhere, bodies in the streets, no infrastructure. They are demanding security and logistical support, but we are still rationing water, for Christ's sake. They have been waiting out the genocide in clean and comfortable hotels in Nairobi and now they're complaining that their rooms are dirty. We take some pleasure from seeing their faces when we invite them to dine with us on the revolting expired German half-rations (which my executive assistant had dubbed "Schweineshite") we have been surviving on for weeks.

---

*   Now the Democratic Republic of Congo.

UN headquarters in New York is increasing its demand for reports and information; the absolutely impossible, wasteful, and ineffective peacetime pace we'd had to deal with before the war is back with a vengeance. We are burned out and injured, yet they don't send water, they don't repair the electricity, they don't provide effective reinforcements. Instead, they say, "Okay, the war is over. Let's get back to work," without taking into account what we had just been through. After all the slaughter and desecration, I'm horrified by the expectation that we should resume something called a "normal routine."

Desperately needed Canadian staff officers arrive, but they seem to be expecting an easier ride. Most seem to resent the pace and the nature of the work I demand of them; some are flagrantly insubordinate. I wonder aloud if they are simply here for the mission subsistence allowance that will bump up their pay, a pre-retirement honeypot.

I contact New York several times a day, demanding the troops, supplies and resources we still need so urgently. I'm bending over backward to help every semblance of a journalist who shows up, just in case one of them might be able to influence their governments to act. Same with celebrities, dignitaries and human-rights

activists; I'm hand-holding them all in the thin hope
that they can get us the help we need by shaming the
international community into supporting a reinforced
mission, and by extension us in the field.

I feel like I'm ranting and raving, tilting at windmills.
I am losing control of my mission area to people who
show little respect to those of us who stayed, and who
are at the edge of sanity. Where earlier I had been
getting two to four hours of sleep a night, now I am just
passing out for a few minutes here and there: at my desk,
or leaning against a wall. Sometimes in mid-sentence.

I manage to procure a few goats to bring something
lively into our days. We have been so captured by the
continuous presence of death that these animals
become a symbol of hope and life. But a pack of
dogs, grown feral from months of living on the over-
abundance of human flesh, manage to slip into the
UN compound and attack them. I hear the bleating and
the barking from my office. Without an iota of restraint
or second thought, I grab my pistol, race outside,
shoving people out of my way. I fire my entire clip.

I don't hit the dogs or any of my troops—thank God.
But my total disregard for protocol and fire-discipline
leaves them staring at me in shock.

My new executive assistant, Phil Lancaster, a friend from my years at the NATO base in Germany in the 1970s, can see more than anyone that I am losing my grip. Years later he wrote to me about that time. "*Mon général*," he began, "I have no idea what was going on in your head but I could clearly see signs of exhaustion and mental lapses. It was not easy watching you struggle on so desperately long past the point when a normal man would have caved in or run away. But, looking back, the things I remember most were the soft words, the little kindnesses—like your insistence that every lovesick Bangladeshi officer have access to your phone after hours so he could spend ages gushing like a teenager to his fiancée back home—and the concern that seemed directed at everyone but yourself. As I said, it was not easy to watch."

Unbeknownst to me, Phil makes a call to UN headquarters, pleading with the military adviser at the UN Department of Peacekeeping Operations (DPKO), my old comrade General Maurice Baril, to get me out before I crash and burn. He feels like a traitor, and I feel like a failure when I make that same call, requesting the unheard-of: to be relieved of my command. But both of us feel an overriding sense of duty to protect the mission and the troops still serving with us. We know both will suffer if the force commander falls apart. And it is clear, now, that this is inevitable.

Lack of sleep, lack of nutrition, an overload of stress, and the effects of the anti-malaria drug* I am taking are affecting me adversely. Still, it takes weeks to convince my superiors that I need to be relieved of command. During that time, I create a detailed continuity plan that includes strongly recommending that my deputy commander, Ghanaian Brigadier-General Henry Anyidoho, replace me as force commander. He is a fellow graduate of the United States Marine Corps Staff College, he knows all the players, he has the largest contingent, he has been with me since the beginning, and he is African. He is the ideal choice for this position, and everyone agrees. Everyone, that is, except the Secretary-General, who chooses to replace me with another white Westerner. This is absolutely the

---

* The drug, Mefloquine, affected my eyesight, sleep and frame of mind. It was the preferred anti-malaria medication because it is taken weekly, instead of daily. As early as January 1994, I had been in touch with Ottawa to say this drug was affecting my ability to function, and I wanted to stop taking it. Their response was that my doing so would be considered a self-inflicted wound: a chargeable offence. When I returned to Canada, I fought the Canadian Forces' medical people to get troops posted in tropical countries off this drug. It took a few years, but they finally did confirm that the side effects were such that troops should stop taking it.

wrong decision, and yet another battle I will not win against the powers that be.

I'm waiting to fly out of Rwanda on August 19. The plane was damaged coming in, and they are repairing the front of the wing with some scraps of metal and duct tape. As I wait on the tarmac where so much history transpired, I recall the many times brave crews had flown in under fire at all hours to sustain the only logistical and humanitarian relief and medevac capability for my mission. The mere sound of those Herc engines inspired us to push into the cross-fire to save so many.

Now, I'm struck by the calm. There are no crowds, no blood, no mad rush for food or medical supplies, no casualties to evacuate, no media clamouring for a story. Just the Canadian Hercules aircraft, waiting to take me away.

In a near trance, I stand on that runway for the last time. I feel as if I have always been in Rwanda; as if I'd just spent my life here. I can't quite grasp the fact that I am leaving, that I won't be coming back. Certainly not in uniform. I have given up my command and I wonder how the hell I will lead my life after this. The guilt of abandoning my troops before the mission is over, the guilt over the Rwandans I feel that I have failed, the loss of my ability to command, our failure to protect, to affect the course of events, to accomplish the mission: these are crushing. I think about the death and martyr-dom of so many innocent Rwandans, the human suffering, the horrific waste. Where was the Creator in all this? Even He had abandoned this place.

When we land in Nairobi, I'm shocked by the normalcy of it all. I feel conspicuous and out of place. For one thing, I am dirty: I haven't had a shower since June. This is mid-August. We had been rationing the little water we had to *drink*; if we wanted a wash, we used a puddle. There was a small, gravel-topped roof outside my deputy's office window where rainwater would sometimes pool—slimy, with all kinds of stuff growing in it. We used that if we wanted to clean our teeth or hands.

The opulence and safety of my Nairobi hotel, in contrast, seems bizarre. I have just come out of hell, with all the smells and noise and destruction, and blood—lots and lots of blood—but here life is normal. How is it possible that the deprivation and death, the odour of rotten flesh, burnt skin, blood and decay so thick you breathed it in, didn't permeate everywhere? It had been as tangible as a membrane. And yet here life goes on as usual, freely, as though unconscious of the

horror that has been unfolding for months just
miles away.

I fly out of hell, injured in body and mind, unable to
fathom a place or time of safety. I land into ignorance,
waste, greed and selfishness.

Accompanied by the immobilizing pain in my neck, shoulder
and arm, I left Nairobi for a mandated two weeks' leave with my
wife and three children. Two weeks of supposed rest and recu-
peration, after a year of adrenalin, chaos and human destruction
that defied description. Two weeks to return to the living and
supposedly forget the dead.

My wife, Beth, heard about my release through the media,
because my communications had been down and no one in
the Canadian military had thought to let her know. She quickly
packed up the kids and, together, we toured the old battlefields
of France. We walked in the sand of the D-Day beaches, where
my father had come ashore under fire fifty years earlier. I ate
fresh food, drank clean water, smelled the scent of flowers on
the breeze. Everything was so clean. Everyone said how glad
they were that I was safe, that it was over, that things were back
to normal. That word again.

They were happy I wasn't wounded, and as far as they knew,
I wasn't. Could they not already see my uneasiness, my edginess,
my constant uncomfortable urge to be ready to react or to retreat
into myself? I remember talking to people and playing with the
kids, so I guess no one noticed, but everything during that trip
took place in a kind of surreal haze. I couldn't truly enjoy it; it
wasn't possible. It just didn't compute. The fatigue, combined

with the discovery that this normalcy still existed, made me sort of a zombie.

My arm was still out of commission, and the pain excruciating. Over the next weeks and months, I would go through all sorts of tests, and the doctors would find absolutely nothing wrong. The paralysis eventually ebbed, as did the phantom pain, but I was left with the feeling that both my mind and my body had taken an awful kicking.

It was clear to me that I was no longer myself, but it was also very plain, right from the start, that everyone expected me to be the same person who had got on a plane to Africa a year ago. So at first I did try to bring myself back, be the man I'd been. Even I didn't know he was gone for good.

My leave was cut short when I was called back to UN headquarters in New York for a debriefing. The family and I landed at Mirabel Airport in Montreal late in the evening. I certainly hadn't been expecting a parade, but military tradition generally makes it a point of honour to have senior officers greet returning troops of any rank, welcoming them back into the fold after being tested in the theatre of operations. But no one was there except for a driver in the empty hall. For the past year, I had led the United Nations Peacekeeping Force in Rwanda through the worst mass atrocity since the Holocaust, during which time I had had sole responsibility for establishing security in an entire country. And here I was, stepping off a plane as if I was returning from a vacation.

Beth, the daughter of an old military family, voiced her opinion of this slight to me very clearly. It looked like my father had been right twenty-five years earlier when I left for the military college in Saint-Jean, Quebec. He'd said, "Son, you are joining a service, and do not expect anyone to say thank you."

So I brushed my feelings aside and arranged for the driver to take my wife and children home to Quebec City, while I stayed at a hotel near the airport. That night, I felt a terrible vacuum beginning to form. I managed to brush that aside, too, but I did not sleep. A few hours later I was on a plane to New York.

My original executive assistant in Rwanda, Brent Beardsley, was there to meet me. Brent had been with me from the start of the mission and through the first month of the genocide, then had fallen gravely ill and had to be evacuated. He'd been in hospital, and then had spent two months' leave at home with his family; he was looking so much better than when I last laid eyes on him. I saw my own reflection in his reaction when he first saw me. I knew I had lost a lot of weight, and most of my hair and moustache had turned white. He came forward to grasp my hand, but the arm paralysis prevented me from returning his greeting.

"Christ, sir," he said. "You look like shit."

He'd always been blunt.

Together, we leapt back into battle mode. The genocide was over, but there was still a mission to complete. Millions of Rwandans— innocents and belligerents alike—were now living in Zaire where tensions were at an explosive level. It was up to us to convince the UN to put a stop to what would eventually become a series of wars that still rage today.

I was jet-lagged and exhausted, but driven, even optimistic. Rwanda had been a disaster, yes, but we had an opportunity right now to take what we'd learned from it and do better. For weeks I had been working on a proposal for an expanded UN mission into Zaire to help the millions of surviving Rwandans return home safely and help them rebuild the country. The reasoning was clear: if we don't do this, Rwanda will have no peace; the belligerents will gain control of the refugees, and it will all

happen again. I explained to everyone who would listen how ineffective the current level of support was, and the desperate need
for international engagement. I spoke with everything that was in
me. I spelled it out as clearly as I could, knowing that the situation in Zaire was an opportunity to make up in some part for my
failure in Rwanda as well as the failure of the entire international
community.

Of course, the one person who should have interviewed me
at the time never did. As the Secretary-General of the United
Nations, Boutros Boutros-Ghali had imposed centralized control
over the information that was reaching the Security Council. So
my sitreps from the field went through him and not directly to the
Security Council. During those critical weeks at the start of the
war, he decided what, if anything, the nations of the world would
learn about the situation in Rwanda. They learned nothing,
so they did nothing. He was the key to those decisions, but his
reasons for not passing my reports on to the Security Council
remain secret to this day.

He didn't even make the pretence of wanting to meet with me.
That was a real slap in the face. Others, like Kofi Annan, who was
then the head of the Department of Peacekeeping Operations,
were effusive in their expressions of respect for my standing firm,
alone, but the main man stayed away completely.

Still, I was encouraged when my briefing to the peacekeeping
staff garnered a standing ovation. My presentation to the troop-
contributing nations, however, had a more complicated recep-
tion. As I described the genocide, and the conditions of the
refugees, many were in tears. But they greeted my proposal for
action and my analysis of the potential consequences of inaction
impassively. When I was finished, the French ambassador stood
up to address the assembly. I tensed, awaiting his response.

The minute he started speaking, I knew there would be no mission. Like so many had before him, the ambassador shot down my plea and my plan to help the people of this tiny African nation. It was too much, he said. Too dangerous, too much risk. I looked around the room, and the representatives from all the countries who had refused to help me stop the genocide were nodding their heads in agreement even as they were wiping away their tears. They did not want to take casualties. Not for this. Not for the people of Rwanda, still dying by the thousands in Goma, in Bukavu, and in displaced-persons camps all over the country.

I had failed to convince them before, and I failed to convince them now.

Brent, a friend as well as a comrade, knew how dark my thoughts were turning. He pulled me aside. "Sir, you could have packed up a Herc-load of bodies, flown it to New York, and dumped it right here on the floor, and it wouldn't have made any difference. Except you would have been charged with the illegal use of an aircraft."

His words simply passed through me. At the time I couldn't hear the sense of them.

Rwanda, January 1994

There are killings around the country, groups of children gang-raped, strangled and left to rot: messages we can't fully decipher. But these horrible and upsetting acts intensify my strong suspicions that a menacing shadow force is at play. I'm pushing my troops to their limits as I attempt to strategize for what is clearly unfolding, while still supporting the peace process between the Rwandan government and the rebel army, the Rwandan Patriotic Front, hunkered north of the demilitarized zone. My frustration level is mounting. I have untrained and ill-prepared troop contingents from several countries, and my requests for stores as well as a promised anti-landmine programme and resources for the demobilization process are all being ignored by New York.

Finally, the missing piece of the puzzle appears. After weeks of suspicions, we now have solid evidence of a planned large-scale massacre from a well-placed and credible informant. He tells us of Interahamwe cells around the country making lists of Tutsis in their communities, so that when the call comes over Rwandan hate radio to destroy the *inyenzi* ("cock-roaches"), death squads will be turned loose on the population. He explains the training they have been receiving, and details the caches of weapons— machetes, clubs, spears, as well as machine guns and grenades. He tells us exactly where to find them. He tells us of a planned ambush on Belgian soldiers near the Presidential Guards' compound. He gives us every-thing we need to put a stop to the whole damn thing before it starts. All he asks in return is that we exchange his Rwandan money for US dollars, and that he and his family receive passports and safe passage to any friendly Western nation.

Brent and I are both trembling with excitement—we finally have a chance to seize the initiative from the belligerents. As I order preparations to raid the arms caches, we carefully craft a code cable—which later became known as the "genocide fax." We had been sent in to Rwanda as a Chapter Six Peacekeeping Mission. Chapter Six of the UN Charter deals with the peaceful settlement of disputes, meaning we are not authorized to collect intelligence or fire a weapon except in self-defence or to protect UN personnel and installations. The existence of the weapons caches, however, are a violation of the peace accord we were there to uphold, and my terms of engagement allow me to act in self-defence and to prevent crimes against humanity. My code cable therefore spells out the impending threat and informs the DPKO of the immediate actions I intend to take. We are confident that we can still turn this around and prevent a massive slaughter.

We are dismayed by the response, received by code cable first thing the next morning.

Absolutely not.

WAITING FOR FIRST LIGHT   19

The chain of command emphatically restates the
limits of our mission: we are to monitor only. This is a
direct order to stay within the narrow boundaries of a
Chapter Six Peacekeeping Operation; only a Chapter
Seven mission allows for action against acts of aggression. I will receive no additional troops, no ammunition,
nothing to forestall the massive human atrocity that is
most certainly about to take place.

I am in disbelief. All I have here in Kigali is an
inexperienced UN civilian staff and a disparate force of
peacekeepers, including the contingent from Belgium,
the former colonial power in Rwanda. There is no
question that I need UN support for an updated mission
and the resources to execute it.

As I read the response again, I know that despite my
lifetime of military training, following this order without
question is impossible. Clearly, I have not properly
explained the situation; we *must* save these people from
a hideous fate. There must be another way to persuade
the UN to take action and give me the tools to intervene.

I spend days making call after call, sending code
cables one after another, arguing for the need to raid the
arms caches, for stopping this thing before it starts.
Eventually even I realize my arguments are futile, so I

order defensive stores and materials for protective
shelters for the people I know we'll end up harbouring.
I order anti-riot gear, as we are already facing unruly
and violent crowds on a daily basis. I do anything I can
to prepare for what I know is coming. But I don't get
anything. Not even a response. Over and over, I try and
I try. And over and over I fail to convince.

"It's been a goddamn nightmare, Roméo, you have *no* idea!"

I was being escorted to meet the commander of the Canadian
army by a senior staff officer who strode quickly along the glossy
granite hallway of the Land Force Command* headquarters, briefing me on the situation here in Saint-Hubert, Quebec. It was my
first day back in the office, just four weeks since I left Rwanda.
Colleagues we passed greeted me with a cheerful "Welcome
back!" or a teasing "Nice of you to drop in!" I responded to each
of them with a stupid chuckle, unable to speak.

"It's been flat-out crisis mode," he continued. "Budgets
slashed to hell—I mean a third right off the top! The Somalia
shit-storm exploding in our faces, the general officer corps a
laughingstock over expense claims. And the media's riding us
hard, scrabbling for scandal like a bunch of goddamn rats. All
I can say is, thank God you're back from your trip! Must have
been something, though—a year-long junket in Africa. Hey, did
you see any elephants?"

---

* The terms were changing around that time. Force Mobile Command had
  become Land Force Command, which is now simply the Canadian Army.

We arrived at the commander's office, and my escort smiled at me. "Time to get to work; you're back in the real world, sir!"

I stood at the door, trying to reconcile his words—the obliviousness of this "real world"—with the reality I had just known.

Rwanda, November 1993

"The first supply shipment's arrived, sir. And you're not going to bloody well believe this."

I raise my eyes to meet Brent's. We had been waiting for weeks for these supplies. In my previous field ops I would be sent off with material to conduct operations, and everything, from toilet paper to tanks, would be replenished automatically. That was the NATO system, a push system that anticipated needs and deficiencies and moved supplies forward based on historic usage. The UN, on the other hand, works on a pull system that expects you to start from zero; once you are on the ground, you make your requests. Then they send out calls for bids, analyze the results, select a vendor, make the purchase, and ship your supplies to the field. This works reasonably well when troops from rich countries are part of your operation and come loaded with the required sixty days' worth of resources. But when you have countries such as Bangladesh and Ghana contributing troops, as we do here, they land empty-handed, without even food for their first meal upon arrival.

The mission's chief administrative officer (CAO) believes that troops should live in tents, but that civilian UN staff have to be afforded regular lodging. He's responsible for all the logistics resources, and he doesn't work under me, so I have no control over major factors that affect my troops. This is an outright sin in military operations.

Brent is holding a battered cardboard box, flaps open. I peer in. Flashlights. He laughs, and says, "But no batteries, sir." I go and see the CAO. His response? "Well, you didn't ask for batteries."

I'm beginning to realize the extent of the logistical problems we are going to face while facilitating this peace process. I don't even have enough radios to stay in touch with the people I am deploying. The radios I do have are insecure non-crypto civilian Motorolas, easily monitored by all sides.

My operational capabilities are grossly limited, too, by a lack of vehicles. The vehicles are here, but civilian staff have first call on them, so they sit all day in the HQ parking lot while the staff sit at their desks. Meanwhile, I don't have means to transport my troops.

Musing on the skewed priorities here, I long for the peak-efficiency outfit I left behind in the Quebec garrison. I radio to request a situation report from the demilitarized zone, only to learn that my colonel there has no paper or pencils to write it with.

Since we've had to start the mission from scratch, I'm spending 70 percent of my time on logistics, instead of at the operational level. I need to be out visiting the troops and discussing details of their deployment plans, but my deputy won't be arriving for another two months, so instead I am running around scrounging, stealing and cajoling, trying to influence the system to get us food and basic supplies, not to mention ammunition for potential self-defence.

The Special Representative to the Secretary-General of the UN is the civilian mission head, and I, as force commander, am the number two. Frustratingly, he orders me to deploy my troops to protect UN sites, instead of the tactical areas that I deem essential. His closest political adviser is a civilian who's also close to the Rwandan president's political party. My operational work is being further curtailed by the need for me to be involved heavily in the political process and negotiations.

I have staff in headquarters who don't even speak

English, let alone the French or Kinyarwanda spoken here. The Ghanaians have no trucks, and their equipment is still on ships somewhere trying to make its way to Rwanda. It never does arrive. During a short visit to Kigali, the Bangladesh chief of defence staff informs me that the reason he committed troops to Rwanda was to mature them in an operational theatre: in other words, to *begin* their field training. The Belgian troops, who are supposed to be my best equipped and best trained, bring broken-down vehicles that have just gone through the wringer in Somalia, and they are using up the little ammo we have in training for their annual inspection, which is scheduled for when they get home. Worst of all, some of them (fully armed and drinking steadily) are discovered by my staff in a local bar boasting about their ability to "kick nigger ass in Africa." As I jump to inform them I will tolerate *no* racism, colonial attitudes, or abuse of power, I know we are not off to a great start.

My initial reaction to coming home was shock. The shock of discovering that what had happened in Rwanda, what was happening still, had absolutely no consequences or importance here. I couldn't believe that the world had neither imploded as a result of the genocide nor risen up in some glorious rebellion against evil. It was as if I had woken from a horrible dream; but it *hadn't* been a dream. Work, home, all just the same.

It kept catching me by surprise, coming as it did from every angle: *You're back, so hop right into your box within the system.* Nobody asked me about the genocide. Nobody even mentioned Rwanda. That's not entirely true: there were a few times. One UN official in New York had a question for me, posed within twenty-four hours of my return to North America: How had I allowed this genocide to happen?

I was also called to a meeting with the prime minister, who greeted me with, "It was terrible, but we know you did your best," and then spent the next fifty minutes reminiscing in French about mutual friends from Shawinigan. We shook hands, a picture was taken, and that was it. That was that.

Though the UN does not request force commanders to provide a mission report or share lessons learned, Brent and I felt it was essential to do so. We spent months on our own, working through the nights to produce a full report detailing the unthinkable brutality, the impotence of the "peacekeepers," the reckless self-interest on the part of the international community and its abandonment of Rwanda, the opportunities missed, and suggestions for future missions.

When I informed the Department of Peacekeeping Operations that we were doing this, their response was swift: no need, no thank you, our staff already put a report together, we have moved on. Between this response and my futile debriefing there, I was left with the firm impression that no one was interested, and the report remained in my files.

Nor did the Canadian government in power or the military hierarchy show any interest in debriefing me on the war or the genocide. Months after I got home, a couple of people from Foreign Affairs took a look at the files I had carried out of my HQ in Kigali, and put the information into a report, which went into a file, which I never saw again.

Later, I gave presentations to the Conference of Defence Associations and the Royal Military College, but there was no request for me to brief the army staff. I found it vexing that the country didn't demonstrate any interest in gaining insights from me for Canada's future engagements.

I did have my one short incoming session with the army commander, Gordon Reay, but he had something else he wanted to discuss. Something I didn't yet understand. Something none of us did.

"We're starting to see some issues with guys coming back from Cambodia and Yugoslavia," he told me. "Fatigue, a few cognitive problems, some trouble readjusting. Nothing more. Nothing to worry about.

"I know you also had a hell of a time, Roméo. What is important is that we need you at the top of your game. We need you to put that work ethic of yours into high gear."

The posting I'd been given as deputy commander of Land Force Command and commander of 1 Canadian Division had been empty for months, and he needed me to attend to all the work that had been left hanging. He told me what he was telling so many others, that it would get easier. He assured me that the best thing for me was to work hard, and with time, it would all disappear. He knew what I had been through, but he repeated the refrain: "You're back in the real world."

And so I worked. For months and years I worked and worked. And nothing disappeared, except for the arm pain. My thoughts, my memories—everything I'd experienced in Rwanda— remained digitally clear, and kept playing out in slow motion in front of my eyes, like a teleprompter.

—

I had been back several weeks. It was late September, and all the crops were in. On the weekend, my wife suggested we go down to the farmers' market by the lovely waterfront in Old Quebec City to get some fresh fruits and vegetables.

It was a cold day, and windy. Although there was a roof over the market, the walls were just plastic strips to cut the wind. We parked the car and walked toward it, chatting, amid a crowd of friendly people. We opened up the plastic sheeting, and I took just a couple of steps when I became completely overwhelmed by the aroma—a sort of sweet, humid smell.

I stared around me at the stalls and the extraordinary colours of the produce—the orange of carrots, the red tomatoes, the green peppers, the strawberries and blueberries. The colours were almost psychedelic. I stopped (well, not me, as I was taking no decisions here). I *was* stopped. Frozen. My feet simply stopped moving. My wife looked at me, wondering what the hell was going on.

Sheer anguish washed over me, and I was suddenly desperate to get out of there. Such a powerful reaction, coming from all that beauty.

As I turned to bolt, it was as if I walked into a memory.

I'm in a marketplace in Kigali—there are women and crying kids sitting on the ground, and in front of them are nearly black bananas, mangoes and squishy, overripe avocados. There is an odour of putrefaction, of rotten-ness. My ears fill with the sound of crying. A crude distribution point has been set up, but it is very disorganized. A truck arrives with big bags of grain. It is cow corn—not rice or wheat—and it has been sent as food aid; however, no one has tools to grind it or pots to cook it in anymore. It is so jagged, the kernels rip open the digestive tracts of anyone who tries to eat it raw. The food aid is literally killing starving children.

The people haven't been properly organized by the NGO to line up and take turns, so they rush the truck. They are ripping at the bags and climbing over each other to fill their little plastic bowls with whatever they can get. It's like piranhas going after an animal carcass; within minutes there is nothing left. The truck is empty and the massive crowd with people yelling and children crying is gone, except for the bodies on the ground—a couple of women and three children, trampled to death.

I ran for the car, and stayed there.

In September 1994, I posted to my new job at army headquarters in Saint-Hubert. Turned out, the Department of National Defence and the Canadian Forces *were* in a crisis (though I had trouble reconciling that word with what I had just lived through). We were escalating missions—with thousands being deployed all over the globe at a pace we hadn't seen for decades—at the same time as our budget was being slashed by a third. The result of this untenable equation was that troops were being put in harm's way. We were throwing thirty thousand people out of the Forces in order to make the budget cuts, we were closing bases—even my own college had been shut down. My job as deputy commander made me the army resource manager, and so I was trying to juggle the impact of all of this on our remaining troops. The daily escalation of duties and responsibilities was unrelenting. And then, thrown in for good measure? The massive "shit-storm" that was the "Somalia affair."

In 1993, two members of the Canadian Airborne Regiment deployed to the peacekeeping mission in Somalia had brutally beaten, tortured and killed a civilian teenager. Disgusting and disgraceful events were uncovered during the investigation, which destroyed the morale and reputation of the Canadian military internationally and domestically. Brutal initiation tactics had apparently become commonplace, and rampant white-supremacist ideology was also found to be entrenched in the elite unit. Blame was falling, rightly, on the shoulders of the leadership as much as on the individual soldiers.

As it turned out, there was not one aspect of my new job and the military overall that wasn't dominated by the fallout of the Somalia mess, despite attempts by some to minimize it or even cover it up. Public outrage had prompted the government to insist on a commission of inquiry, and when it was set to start, the chief of defence staff told me I would be the first witness. Because I had been out of the country and not involved in Somalia, he wanted me to be the one to explain to the commission how we train and develop leadership skills in the officer corps and also, to a lesser degree, the non-commissioned officer (NCO) corps.

Soon, in addition to my own work, I was being urged on one side by three-stars at National Defence headquarters in Ottawa to take action on the investigations, and berated on the other side by army colleagues assuring me the whole affair had been an isolated incident.

It was clear to me that we were in a leadership crisis. There was no intellectual rigour to any training we were doing. We were in a new era of conflict, so different from classic war, but all we had was hand-me-down experiential knowledge from the Second World War and Korean War vets to go on; we were the third and fourth generation learning from these same war stories and examples. There'd been no new guidance on military leadership since the early 1960s.* There had been no reviews or adjustments or analysis conducted on changing operational requirements and social structures, nor had anyone given serious consideration to the fact that changing demographics were providing the army with a significantly different recruit. Our ranks were no longer filled with youth from rural areas with intrinsic knowledge of the rugged outdoors of the farm or the bush; we were sending city kids out to the field with training based on an earlier generation's basic life skills. They didn't even know how to stay warm in the snow, much less how to stay cool in the desert or the jungle.

The soldiers had changed, as had war itself: it was no longer a matter of superpowers meeting each other on the field of battle,

---

* To be fair, General Dextraze, the chief of defence staff, was a solid war veteran who had written a letter on leadership in 1972. The major problems the American forces were facing at the time—with the Vietnam War, drug use and other problems—were having a knock-on effect in Canada. So the general had felt it necessary to restate what our role as fighting soldiers meant, using the Second World War as the exemplary model. This old soldier had not realized how significantly the world had changed, and yet his letter was the only guidance on leadership provided to the military during this very significant time of turmoil.

but a new world disorder. We were Cold War warriors ready to fight huge armoured forces in Central Europe, hoping that these small, intra-state kerfuffles were just a passing phase. But we were no longer facing classic war, or even classic peacekeeping: in this new style of warfare civilians, even women and children, are not only *on* the front line, they *are* the front line. The Somalia mission was able to degenerate the way it did because our training had not adapted to these new realities.

How was I going to reconcile the directive to extol our leadership training with the truth?

The deputy chief of defence staff called me up to tell me that we had twenty-six cases of people accused of wrongdoing in Somalia, but the commander of the army was dragging his heels. He wanted me to sort this out immediately. I could just picture it: the commander, smoking in his office, saying, "Well, you know, boys will be boys." Much of the army leadership (in contrast to the Canadian Forces leadership) had their heads in the sand, refusing to admit there was a breakdown of leadership philosophy and its application that was directly responsible for this rogue regiment. They were insisting that the whole affair could be attributed to the actions of a few bad apples who went a bit overboard in a difficult situation.

I was not playing to this tune. I had just come out of command in the field, and knew the things my troops and I had gone through. Somalia had been difficult, yes, and the conditions harsh, certainly, and some excellent work had been accomplished by the Canadian contingent; however, the actions of some of the Canadian troops and the subsequent inaction from the various levels of leadership were unacceptable. There was no goddamn way anyone could say this was just a few guys not following the rules.

It was a crisis that required a draconian solution. And so I recommended that we disband the source of the Somalia debacle,
the whole Airborne Regiment—just pack up the parachutes for
a few years, and move those troops to flesh out other regiments.
I believed it was essential to spread them throughout the army, and
get them back into the standard, straight-leg soldiering. I believed
that the ethos of our profession was still present in the core of the
army and especially in the regimental system. Infantry battalions
were being drastically reduced, and the numbers were too low to
be effective. By disbanding the Airborne Regiment and its support
elements, we would help boost infantry numbers and also dis-
tribute some of the advanced tactical skills that the Airborne had
acquired over the years. And most important, the Airborne guys
would be reacquainted with proper behaviour and leadership
in those standard units. This direct address of the source of the
scandal would also appease the public and our political masters,
and help us hit budget targets. And if in the future we found that
we needed a parachute regiment, we could revive it after memories had faded in the public and political realms.

The Department of National Defence was in the process of
restructuring the entire Forces, and so had requested army staff
to write a draft proposal for a restructuring of Land Forces, which
was now making the rounds inside army HQ. I added my detailed
recommendation for the Airborne to it. Surprisingly, it never
came back to me for final review, but went directly from the chief
of staff to the commander (both of whom were ex-Airborne). By
the time it got to National Defence headquarters, my suggestion
had been cut from the proposal.

To say I was disappointed would be an immense understate-
ment. The disconnect between the acknowledgement of a crisis

and the overt disregard by those in positions of authority was disturbingly familiar. Shades of Rwanda.

Rwanda, April 1994

The security situation is rapidly worsening. I spend all my time prepping, arguing, and seeking resources for what I know is coming.

On the night of April 6, the situation literally explodes: the president of Rwanda's plane is shot down and everyone on board is killed. This is clearly some sort of signal: *Go*. Bloody slaughter erupts across Kigali in a matter of hours.

Within the first full day, ten of my troops, all Belgian, and hundreds of Rwandan Tutsis are massacred. My compounds are soon sheltering at least fifteen thousand terrified civilians, and the numbers increase by the hour. My protection enclosures are bursting at the seams. We have no electricity, no tarps to shelter people in the stadium from the elements, no firewood, no water, no food for any of them. They are saved, only to face starvation. Many of my troops give up their meagre rations; they will not eat in front of hungry children. There are no supplies forthcoming. No reinforcements. No decisions.

I'm racing around to all the major players trying to persuade them to stand down, getting nowhere. Evidence of the slaughter is littered through the streets: bodies lying on the side of the road with their heads split open.

Sixteen hundred troops arrive from France and Belgium, and the United States Marine Corps is on a ship just off the coast, but all of them are here to rescue expatriates. *Not* to assist me in curtailing the killings and chaos now gripping the capital.

Friday evening comes and nearly everything stops at UNHQ in New York for the weekend. There will be no cavalry coming over the hill. Of course, war takes no weekends. Thousands of Rwandans are murdered in the streets: first with grenades and guns, then by machetes and clubs.

I have zero capacity to protect my own troops, as we are drastically short of ammunition and heavy weapons; the defensive stores we requested don't arrive. And I am in an even more helpless situation, unable to guarantee protection for the civilians streaming into my compounds. But still they come by the thousands, relying only on our moral credentials: that UN sites, like churches and schools, are protected against attack under international law.

Within a few days, I am protecting over 32,000 Rwandans of both ethnic groups in my compounds, as code cables pour in from the UN telling me that I have no authority to do so.

Orders come in from the national capitals of the nations who have troops in the mission to pull their soldiers, and the UN Secretary-General acquiesces. I receive my own order to pull out, and I go straight to my deputy commander, Henry. I inform him of the order, and tell him that I plan to defy it. I ask him if he and his contingent from Ghana are willing to stay with me—to follow an illegal order in a risky situation. Without hesitation, he tells me that they will not run away. He is a great man, and a great officer.

Very soon, my mission is reduced to barely four hundred troops on the ground. I've been cut adrift with these brave souls, with no one willing to come and help stop this genocide.

I abandon my quarters and camp out in my office. I never remove my uniform. Brent finds me the occasional can of Schweineshite or a bar of chocolate, and a pillow. Each night I sit down at my desk, knowing that day more and more Rwandans had been murdered and that my mission had been unable to stop the slaughter.

At daybreak each morning I radio the two most vulnerable locations my troops are guarding—the King Faisal Hospital and the Hôtel des Mille Collines, both located deep in Kigali and high-value targets for the extremists to wipe out—dreading that my soldiers will not answer. Each day the killings accelerate. The smells and screams invade our premises, even the pores of our skin. In churches, in hospitals, in schools, Tutsis have been segregated under the guise of protection and then systematically slaughtered. The extremists have a total disregard for any international law; their actions mock the Geneva Conventions. My compounds remain secure merely because I bluff that we have the backing of the entire international community, but there is a constant threat that my men, who have no ammunition for their weapons, will simply be cut down, and the extremists will wipe out everyone we've been protecting.

Thankfully, the remaining troops, all (except a dozen Canadian officers who rushed in to help just as everyone else was obeying the order to leave) from small and poor nations, commit themselves nobly to our cause. The small detachment of Congolese observers are courageously and cleverly using bluffs and misdirection to prevent the extremists from getting at the Tutsis in the Mille Collines. The Ghanaians are holding on to the airport, which is vital for humanitarian relief and support of my force. The Tunisians are guarding the hospital, which now looks more like a concentration camp; a mortar projectile has exploded, and children have been trampled in the survivors' rush to get away.

While these images are seared in my brain, they are images of war, for which I have been thoroughly trained. It is something else that begins to play havoc with my mind: the horrible realities of my futile command. I simply cannot keep everyone safe—the threat is so massive and my troops so few. Several times an hour, I have to make decisions that mean some will live and others will not. Sometimes I'm not able to get forces there in time, or the risk is simply too high.

We are receiving constant calls from UNHQ, from governments, from NGOs, even from the Vatican, telling us that the troops sent in to save expatriates hadn't managed to evacuate such-and-such a person, and that we need to rescue them. For a few days I put my troops in danger for these privileged few. But driving past Rwandans being slaughtered in order to save some Westerners is just too much. It is unethical and inhumane, and goes against every moral reference I've ever had. Brent looks like he wants to throw the phone through the window every time it rings with another special request. "This stops now," I decide. It's time to concentrate on saving the most vulnerable, not the most white or the most elite.

Then I am struck by how this decision, and thousands of others, forces me to play God with people's lives. This non-stop series of direct decisions isn't just affecting my troops—I have spent a lifetime preparing for the possibility of sending them into harm's way, and they know the risks they face in any operational theatre—but innocent civilians. The almost-omnipotent position I am in is horrifying; a lose-lose dilemma. Each time I give a command that will save a life, I condemn someone else to mutilation and death.

Yet I am the solitary source of protection for these desperate people, these few tens of thousands, out of hundreds of thousands being slaughtered, and millions suffering injury, disease, terror and displacement. I am well aware that the United Nations is not giving me the authority to protect any of them—I am to protect UN personnel and UN assets only.

Everything I am doing is against the rules of my official mandate, in direct contradiction of my stated mission, but there is no more peace to keep.

And so I write my own mission as I go. It is perhaps this combination of split-second, ethical dilemmas that causes the first firecracker to go off in my head. There will be many more over the next three months.

My first week back, I was invited to go to Niagara Falls to make a keynote address to the Infantry Association. I agreed because the organizer had been a subordinate of mine for years, and I was happy to do him this small favour.

It was not a pleasure trip, though they agreed that I could bring my wife. The two of us flew to Toronto the night before, arriving very late, and then drove to the meeting first thing in the morning. I gave the presentation, and we drove straight back to Toronto to catch the flight home that afternoon; we never even saw the falls. I really wanted to minimize my time away from the kids.

A scandal soon erupted around my expenses for this trip. National Defence had approved my travel, but my wife's fare was to be paid by the Infantry Association. However, the DND clerk mistakenly put Beth's fare on my claim, and I (like the commander on *M*A*S*H* signing everything Radar O'Reilly put in front of him) mindlessly signed off.

To put this into context, at the time, brown envelopes (secret insider tips, both authentic and fabricated, leaked to journalists) were flying, accusing generals of profligate spending while the troops were having a hard time making ends meet. The budget cuts had caused a revolution around thinking about privilege and rank. Where senior and general officers had once enjoyed certain perks, now they had become fair game; at any hint of special privilege or abuse of our scant resources (founded or not), the media pounced.

My expense claim was fed to a journalist who called me to say he was going to make it public, and did I have any comment. After everything I had lived through in Rwanda, I now had to face not only the offensive suggestion that I had been shirking my real duties (as if Rwanda had been a little side-show), but now that I was pilfering. The intense media investigation of this claim had a grave impact on me. It confirmed to me that life back here at home made absolutely no sense at all. The Infantry Association quickly acknowledged that they had intended to pay for my wife, and that the claim had been a clerical error. But the whole thing sort of blew a fuse in me (how many did I have left to destroy?).

Looking back, it's difficult for me to figure out why I didn't just tell my bosses to go screw themselves. I mean, the budget problem was theirs, the Somalia affair, the base closures and lack of resources—the whole mess. And yet I kept working. More than that, I did it with dogged stubbornness and devotion. That membrane in the shape of Rwanda—the smell of hate and death and destruction—was always around me. But I knew I was supposed to act as if I'd just done my job. Sure it was a war, but it was still my job, what I was trained for, no big deal. Now let's get back to being a general in Canada.

The worst part was that I felt compelled to fall into that, and to minimize what I had gone through, what Rwanda had endured. At work I felt compelled not to talk about my state of mind, my fatigue and sense of disconnection. I was proud, I guess, of my ability to cope—and sometimes nearly guilty for having been away for a year. The implication was that now I was doing work for real people: Canadians. The unspoken corollary: Rwandans weren't real people. That really ate away at me.

Over the next two years, first as deputy commander of Land Force Command, and then as commander of the Quebec area, I oversaw the unprecedented slashing of support for our soldiers' quality of life: their salaries, their equipment, their training, their time off, their medical treatment, even the few programmes and services for this new generation of injured veterans. Everything that would show the fighting troops a modicum of respect for their willingness to lay their lives on the line was cut by a third. I oversaw these same soldiers as they were being sent around the globe to serve in complex peacekeeping missions at a tempo we hadn't seen in forty years. I juggled this dichotomy alongside scandal after scandal (everything from the Somalia affair, to a general who'd been fiddling his expense claims, to one caught poaching a deer out of season; it was non-stop). It felt like the reputation of the Forces and of senior officers like myself were being flushed down the toilet.

Straight out of Rwanda, I had been thrown into this swamp full of alligators. My predecessor had decided to take early retirement, and the position had been empty for months before my arrival. Like him, I was a field commander. I didn't particularly want the job of managing resources for the army during this arduous time, either. It would have been a lot easier to accept some desk job behind the scenes. And yet, since Rwanda, something— everything—inside me seemed to have changed. At that point, I didn't recognize that I'd sustained an injury, but I did realize that something new was driving me. Something that challenged my professional perspective. Something raw that made me ... I don't know ... *care* more.

I noticed a rift in thinking developing between me and my colleagues. For instance, in the growing pains of this new era of conflict, many of them thought humanitarian and non-governmental workers were lightweights who couldn't produce lasting results in the field—that they simply reacted to catastrophes, and then waited for the next one. I had come from that school, too, and my experience in Rwanda should have reinforced this thinking: save for a few brave individuals, the NGO community abandoned the Rwandan people, along with all the development work it had done and the massive amounts of dollars it had spent. The genocide destroyed the schools and infrastructure and wiped out nearly every lawyer and judge in the country. Decades upon decades of international development efforts went up in smoke, or, rather, were washed away in a torrent of blood. And yet I had also seen the importance of their efforts, then and many times since. Their adherence to the tenets of neutrality and humanitarian safe spaces inside a conflict zone created resentment among the military and security forces they relied on to defend them, but NGOs were having a positive effect on the ground and, more and more, represented the voice of humanity in crisis. They were also gaining in their ability to influence public opinion and government policies at home and abroad. We military types just couldn't dismiss them out of hand.

Another military school of thought at the time—a very powerful one—dictated that we not take casualties on humanitarian missions. Ever. In a classic war scenario, of course, the rules are different. In the Second World War, for example, the mission to defeat the enemy was paramount, and loss of troops was the reality of war. In classic peacekeeping—like what we had in Cyprus—we were rarely engaged in fighting; we were merely there to observe, so of course we did not risk soldiers' lives. Since

I was a peacekeeper in Rwanda, it has been argued that the
safety of my troops came first and foremost. But what we ended
up observing was not peace, but mass atrocities. Did I not then
have an ethical obligation to change the nature of my mission, a
responsibility to protect? While I carry the burden of the loss of
life that resulted from my command decisions (both among my
troops and the Rwandan people), the ethical mission of protection did and will always come first. Most of my colleagues vehemently disagreed. Fundamentally, they argued, humanitarian
missions do not call for risking the lives of our troops.[*]

I could no longer muster the cynicism to adhere to either of
these outdated military mindsets. But neither could I abandon
the military. I carried on, and committed myself to formulating
solutions to the problems facing us and negotiating compromises.
Those of us in the Forces who acknowledged the problems were
madly trying to fix what was broken and unravelling in our hands.
As so often in my life, the ethos and collegiality of the military
also buoyed me up and kept me going.

Off duty, however, was a different story.

My family had lived in Quebec City military quarters while I was
in Rwanda. Now that I was back, my wife preferred to stay on
there, even though I was posted two and a half hours away (first to
Saint-Hubert and then to Montreal). She felt that the three kids
were well-established in good private schools, and didn't want to
disrupt that or their relationships with good friends. Also, she had
her elderly mother and two sisters close by, so she felt it was best

---

[*] It is important to note that the introduction of the responsibility to protect
(R2P) doctrine in the UN *has* opened up security forces mandates to incorporate the protection of civilians, though this did not happen for another
ten years (2005).

for the family overall if I travelled to them from my places of duty, rather than uproot them all to be with me.

This caught me a bit off guard, but many of my colleagues were in the same boat, and I understood the reasoning behind it. Everyone on the home front had had a tough time while I was away. There had been enough international media coverage that my young family had lived the genocide in real time, too. TV, social media, Skype and cell phones make this the bitter new reality for families of soldiers in conflict zones. My wife and kids had also noticed that nobody abroad or back home seemed to give a damn, and this had been incredibly hard for them.

Also difficult for my wife had been the lack of support she had received while I was in Rwanda, both from my side of the extended family and from the military system. Upon my return, my sisters took pains to tell me how stressful the genocide had been for *them*, expressing little concern for me or for my family. Their attitude exposed a rift that had been just under the surface for years and was a direct result of the way we'd been raised. I don't remember love in my childhood. I remember religion. I remember rules and chores. When it came to taking care of me and my sisters, my father would say, "If there is food on the table and the roof's not leaking, I've done my job."

Neither did my wife elicit much empathy from fellow military families while I was away. Because she was married to a general at a time when the rank and file felt the generals were a bunch of fat cats, many thought she would receive extra support; in reality it was just the opposite. Beth came from a military family. She had been raised in that Quebec City garrison; she had gone to school there, taught school there, and then come back to live there with me several times, including the two years before I was sent to Rwanda when I actually commanded the garrison. And yet when she sought information about my well-being from my deputy of those two years, he had his wife inform Beth that she must follow protocol like anyone else and send her requests via the official channels in Ottawa.

The general attitude was why was I still there, in Kigali, taking absurd risks when I should have come back home when the UN ordered me to. For my wife, as well as for me, it had been a difficult, isolating time.

Also, my return was in many ways a disruption for the family, who had learned how to get along without me over the year I was gone. Our time together, just a little over a week when I was relieved of command, and then on weekends over the years to follow, was difficult for them, as well as me. I rarely slept, still running on the adrenalin of the war, and when I did I suffered from night thrashings, sweating and making all kinds of noise, waking up at all hours. In the morning, the bed would be a disaster with sheets and blankets on the floor, pillows everywhere. My days were so focused on adjusting to normal, the nights must have seemed like a time to fight. Of course, it didn't take very long before I was spending those nights on the couch and, later, in a spare room in the basement.

I found myself increasingly intolerant of home life. I felt frustrated with the children for not wanting to eat their peas or whining for a new toy; I disdained simple requests from my wife to help choose a new sofa pattern or to attend a party with friends; I marvelled at the neighbours washing their cars and pruning their gardens. To me it all seemed so unimportant, so materialistic, so wasteful it was almost obscene.

Even the fact that I still *had* a family, when I had seen so many destroyed, felt wrong to me. Similarly, I shied away from non-work social engagements: too many friends I'd made in Rwanda had been slaughtered. I suspect that veterans of any mission experience some or all or even more of this when they return, becoming distant, introspective, unwilling to open up, mistrustful of themselves and others. At last I understood why my father's generation spent their post-war years on barstools in Legion halls. At least there they were understood, and so allowed themselves to be themselves — their new selves.

And yet, even though I knew how difficult I was to live with, I found being separated from the family hard. At least during my first year back, I was fortunate to be housed in the officers' mess, surrounded by the bustle and activity of the army HQ staff and a constant flow of visitors. But the following year, when I was posted to command the Quebec area, I was assigned to a house; again, my family did not join me. I reminded myself that it was for the good of the children, as I rattled around that big empty place in the nights, listening to the silence. I was isolated and longing for someone to talk to, someone to listen.

Again, this is not an unusual situation. It is difficult for all vets of such catastrophic and complex missions to come home and discover that no one really wants to know what they witnessed, what they did. Maybe at first your spouse will listen to you pour your heart out all night long. But the next time, it's only for an hour or two. By the third time, they are interrupting to ask if you remembered to feed the dog or take out the garbage. You are not supposed to grieve too much, or too long. Too often, your friends and loved ones believe you need to forget the whole thing; and the less they know about it, the more they think they are helping you to get over it.

Most soldiers on mission live the experience together and come back together, and can tap that bond. That is not the experience of a general. I came home alone. I know others experience isolation: a reservist who ends up back in her hometown, far from her mission comrades; an officer seconded to the field who comes back to colleagues who are only anxious that he pick up the slack he created by going. For me, as a general, I couldn't talk my situation over with two dozen buddies over a glass of beer the way I would have done in the old days. It would have been inappropriate for me to burden the officers under my command in that way. I still had a responsibility to watch out for them, not have them watch out for me.

Still, I felt a compulsion to tell someone what had happened. It was clear that nobody in a position of influence in the government or military wanted to hear, but I quickly discovered that there were people in the civilian world who wanted to know about Rwanda. When I started receiving invitations to speak at high schools and rotary clubs, bowling leagues and book groups, I said yes. Every time.

Soon, I was giving three or four lectures a week.

"This," I said, indicating the image on the projection screen behind me, "is a church outside of Kigali. The extremists had spread the word to the population: 'Don't worry, if you feel you are a target, go to a church and stay there. You will be protected.'"

My voice quickened, words coming out rapid-fire, cruelly matter-of-fact: "Of course, once these places were jam-packed with people, they would close the doors, toss a couple of grenades through the roof, and then go in to finish everyone off. In this church alone, we counted 1,100 bodies. They were not killed by high-tech weapons; they were hacked and slashed by machetes. And after a couple of hours and a couple of beers, I guess it gets pretty tiring hacking and slashing, so they learned quickly not to bother killing outright; but to maim and make people suffer, first. So, at the next church, or schoolhouse, they would hack around the heads, opening wounds that would leak and fester. It would take a day or two for them to die in the heat; thousands of people, piled on top of each other; women and children, dying over days."

With eyes on fire I held up a watermelon, then I pulled out the machete I had brought back with me from Rwanda, and savagely sliced it in two. The crowd gasped, and some cried out. It was terribly vicious on my part, but it seemed to me that words were not enough: I needed people to realize what had actually happened to real human beings. I had to make them know this wasn't just statistics and photos of bodies in a far-off place.

"That level of ruthlessness, and our ability to comprehend . . ." I faltered. "A two-year-old child's arm chopped up on a board, like a hot dog. Women with children on their backs, killing other women with children on their backs. That is the level of indoctrination and fury that can be created in these aimless youth who have been given a cause. That is what we face."

Over and over, I would tell the story. Each time, adding some horrible new detail, digging myself deeper into the memories, so that they might be as tangible for my audience as they were for me. Like the Ancient Mariner, I would hold them with my *glittering eye*, so they *could not choose but hear*. Desperately, I would try to make them understand this, this *hellish thing*.

"And how are we dealing with this?" I would challenge. "Our leaders say, 'You will go to Rwanda for two years and they will have a democratic election and you can pack up and leave.'

"Bullshit!" My expletive echoed in the silent room, shock on the faces in the crowd. *God save thee, ancient Mariner!/From the fiends, that plague thee thus!*

"There is no such thing as short-term solutions in these complex missions, where assistance is so essential. Why should our politicians be impatient? Hey, here with the Quebec referendum facing us, we are living a political situation that may nearly destroy our country, but it's a problem that started in 1759. And *we* are impatient for *them* to solve their problems?" I could hear myself shouting now. "Who in the hell are we? Why should *they*—after their history, and the artificiality of their countries, that were created *by us*—all of a sudden in the space of a couple of years be able to wipe that all away and function like a nice, neat North American nation?"

I summoned some control, and calmed my tone. "To transfer their cultures—which are *magnificent* cultures in themselves—to what we consider democratic, is going to take time. So what? As long as it is respectful of human dignity. *That* is the name of the exercise.

"So how have we been doing so far? My estimation is that we are doing terribly. I am convinced that if some idiotic outfit decided it was going to wipe out the 320-odd mountain gorillas that live in the volcanic mountains of northwest Rwanda, the international community would react a lot more rapidly and with a lot more force to protect those gorillas than it did to save the lives of the hundreds of thousands of human beings who were slaughtered in that country, week after week."

Trembling and perspiring, I stared out into the crowd. "Why?

"One day, when I was out on patrol in the thick of the genocide, I came across a little child still living in a hut with the bodies of his dead and decomposing parents. This boy was the same age as my son back home. I looked into his eyes and I saw the eyes of my own son. They were exactly the same. And I knew that this boy was exactly as beautiful and precious and important as my own children. As your own children. Exactly. A Rwandan Patriotic Front patrol came by and took him safely behind their lines; but in my heart, I had already brought him home and added him to my family.

"I think back on that child, and the tens of thousands like him, abandoned, abducted or murdered in the genocide. I think of them whenever an Amber Alert is activated, seeking one missing North American child.

"And it leads me to ask myself, as I ask you today, Are all humans human? Or are some humans more human than others?"

Going full steam at all hours was what had kept me alive in Rwanda, and it felt like it was keeping me alive now. I've always had an extreme work ethic, but now I was stretching that beyond all reason, taking on more and more projects. The heavy workload and the intense speaking schedule were successfully distracting me, but of course they were also dragging me down.

I was not sleeping or taking care of myself. I was not exercising. For thirty years I had done physical training every day, but after Rwanda I lost the will. It was as though I had no compulsion to do anything healthy or positive for myself.

I had lost a lot of weight in Africa. My body was weak from lack of nourishment, but it was also just worn down. Now I found myself cramming down two or three hamburgers, fries, sodas, chocolate bars, until I could feel the pain of my straining stomach. With effort, I would turn my mind away from memories of African rats grown to the size of dogs from gorging on an endless supply of human flesh.

My driver would run out to fast-food joints for me, supplying me with a constant glut of junk food. He understood. He used smoking and drinking to cope. He had been in Sarajevo as a regimental photographer; this poor guy had had to take pictures of buckets of heads and kids nailed to doors. He came back a mess, but his commander rejected the reality of this kind of injury, claiming that under good leadership it just doesn't happen. The impact of that attitude exacerbated the wound. My driver was one of the invisible, the walking wounded, whose injuries it suited the military leadership to deny.

As the Quebec area commander, I had been able to keep this driver to take me to out-of-town meetings and to the garrison in Quebec City where I could see my family on the few weekends I could spare. But as I got into an incredible rhythm of speech-making, he also volunteered to accompany me to each engagement. Over time, I created nearly a hundred overhead-projector slides that I used during my presentations (we didn't have PowerPoint back then), and since he was always with me, he began to help out by flipping the slides for me. Night after night for months and months we would drive God-knows-where and relive the genocide.

I didn't realize the strain this was putting on him, because we were both in it together—working all day, driving for hours, and presenting the horrors of an insanity that had been outside any rules of war we'd been trained for, but which we had lived, and continued to live, in our minds. He had been lost, and by focusing on assisting me he found a way. His loyalty to me was unfaltering. Personally and professionally, he was there for me—bringing me food, assisting with my presentations, driving me around, even playing with my kids, who grew to think of him as an unofficial uncle. He was proud to help, proud to have a métier that made sense to him. It was the same with me and those speeches: they brought me close to the only thing that made any sense to me anymore—the senselessness of the genocide.

Despite this, and although the audiences were clearly interested in the content, I was not getting anything positive out of giving these presentations. They had no constructive effect on me whatsoever. They were taking precious time away from my duties. They were keeping this terrible thing up close and in my face. They were draining me. I would come back from those speeches exhausted, not only from having spoken for hours, but from having spoken with so much emotion. Every time, I relived the experience. Every single time. And then when I was done, I'd sit down to paperwork for a few hours in the night, because I needed to block out what I had just brought back to the surface. I did hundreds of these presentations. Almost nightly, I chose to relive it all. It was as if I was addicted to the pain they caused me.

Those first two years back, I could not divorce myself from Rwanda. I'm not even sure I could say the war was over; I was still living it. I kept two huge filing cabinets, full of my notes, cables, documents and photos, beside my bed. Locked inside, I had the whole genocide. The presence of those files was like something alive, pulsing in the corner, waiting to strike.

CHAPTER TWO

Alone, alone, all, all alone,
Alone on a wide wide sea!
And never a saint took pity on
My soul in agony.

D OCTORS TELL US THAT a trauma left untreated can get worse. Severe mental trauma, much like a deep cut or a malignant tumour, can fester and spread if left to itself, until the entire system is overwhelmed and succumbs. My injury started in Rwanda, but it was exacerbated in Canada. For two years, I blindly worked as it was eating away at my mind and soul, attempting to drown it in an ocean of activity and responsibility. I had no conscious sense during that time that what I had experienced in my last weeks in Rwanda — putting the mission at risk, putting myself at risk, with my behaviour — was still affecting me. I knew I was working myself into the ground, but I also felt I was at the top of my game, pushing the envelope of reform. But as pressures increased, my injury began to make itself known.

Telling and retelling the story of the genocide, and my role in it, became an obsession. I grasped every opportunity to cast myself back to the thousand hills of Rwanda, vowing never to allow the genocide to fade from collective memory. I knew the Rwandan people would never have the resources that, for instance, the Jewish community had gathered to keep the lessons of the Holocaust fresh in people's minds. So I made it my mission to humbly attempt to do this on their behalf. But also, on a more personal level, I felt driven to recount every image seared into my brain so I could sink ever deeper into the pain and the guilt, and be crushed by the weight of hundreds of thousands of souls standing over me in judgement.

No one recognized what I was doing at the time. Not even me. Nobody told me I was injured. I didn't think I was injured, though I felt the weight of having had to ask to be relieved of command. Outwardly, I was still committed, determined, stable. Inwardly, the stresses I was imposing on myself were beating me down, piling up on the stresses at work.

Professionally, the intensity of the budget cuts, the media scrutiny, the flagrant disrespect for the military (and generals in particular), the tempo and complexities of our missions, and their adverse effects on our troops, were compounded by new tensions in Quebec, the area now under my command.

The battle between the Cree First Nation and Hydro-Quebec had begun decades earlier when important Cree land had been appropriated by the province. Now, the power company wanted to start a controversial construction project on that land, and the Cree and their supporters were threatening to blow the whole thing apart. Coming on the heels of the Oka crisis, any government and military dealings with aboriginal communities were both sensitive and tense.

And, at the same time, the entire country was on edge, bracing for a referendum vote that threatened to tear us apart:

on October 30, 1995, the people of Quebec were going to decide whether or not to separate from the rest of Canada. Passions and tempers were flaring around the vote, as were centuries-old animosities and remembered injustices between French and English. As a francophone immersed since birth in the Anglo establishment, I understood both sides, and knew as well as anyone how far the battle over the referendum could go.

I had command of the only federal troops in the province, and began formulating a strategy to prepare for potential turmoil. Pushing aside memories of my futile planning in Rwanda, I thought back to my early days as a young officer commanding troops during the 1970 FLQ crisis, when tensions on the home front were so high and the potential for violence so great. Back then, we had very broad rules of engagement and a lot of discretion as to whether to use force; this was certainly no longer the case. After we had delineated the threats, the risks and the potential for escalation, my staff officers and I formulated a mitigation strategy.

However, in the midst of our preparations, the army commander contacted me with a blunt order not to proceed. There was to be no planning for or even consideration of deploying forces, he told me; no contingency plans or alerts were to be prepared. Nothing was to be said or done that might be leaked to the media and exacerbate the entire debate. The government did not want either side to think the army was going to get involved, and they especially didn't want another October Crisis[*]

---

[*] In October 1970, in response to the kidnapping of British trade commissioner James Cross and provincial cabinet minister Pierre Laporte by the Front de libération du Québec, Prime Minister Pierre Trudeau controversially invoked the War Measures Act, deploying troops through Quebec and Ontario.

on their hands. Yet, I knew that if the shit hit the fan, we would be expected to be there in five minutes.

I felt like I was back in Rwanda: my mission was to provide security, but my orders were not to do so.

My Rwandan wounds were also being re-opened by the negative press I was getting from Europe, as Belgium launched an investigation into the deaths of the ten Belgian peacekeepers who had been deployed to the prime minister's residence at the outbreak of the genocide.* The accusation in the media and in certain military circles, including here in Canada, was that my priority as force commander on that calamitous day should have been protecting my peacekeepers, not trying to stop a civil war and mass slaughter. On and on rolled the Monday-morning quarterbacking of my decisions in Rwanda.

Those critiquing my handling of the mission rarely mentioned the eight hundred thousand slaughtered Rwandans. Or even the four Senegalese, Uruguayan and Ghanaian soldiers with my mission who lost their lives protecting innocent civilians. The deaths they focused on were those of the ten Belgians.

Worse than all of the negative attention on me was the court-martial of Luc Marchal, the Belgian colonel who had been my Kigali sector commander. The Belgian government was determined to punish someone for the deaths of their troops, and since

---

* In the early morning of April 7, 1994, the Belgium patrol had been overwhelmed and disarmed by elite Rwandan government troops, and subsequently killed by a rebellious mob of troops in Camp Kigali who believed it was the Belgians who had shot down the Rwandan presidential plane the night before.

I was out of reach, Luc was the scapegoat. I was determined to do everything I could to defend him. The charges the Belgian authorities were bringing against him were based on erroneous, flawed information, and the court martial was clearly politically motivated. The United Nations was standing firm on my immunity from any such investigation, and the Canadian government took exactly the same position.

But I felt I could not remain silent. The only way I could assist in defending Luc was through a laborious legal process known as Letters Rogatory, through which I could provide evidence without having to appear in person.

I spent weeks and months going through my files and taking extensive advice from legal counsel, and still, before the letters could be submitted, the UN wanted to vet my answers, then sent them back to me with lists of changes. The work was intense, and pulled me even more strongly back into hell than the speeches I'd been giving. Night after night, my lawyers and I waded through piles of paper, verifying facts, chasing supporting documentation, spending endless hours preparing answers to questions, then ripping them up and starting again.

In the end this work proved trebly useful, as the material we prepared was not only relevant for Luc's defence at his court martial, it also supplied enlightening evidence to the various European investigations and the UN-mandated International Criminal Tribunal for Rwanda, to which I was soon to be called as a witness. Trials had been taking place in Arusha, Tanzania, since the end of the genocide. While no one in the international community had wanted to help stop it, once the genocide was over, human rights investigators were sent in, and they recommended a tribunal to identify and prosecute those responsible.

The tribunal had been deposing survivors for many months, and I was to be the first senior official to testify.

In all I spent close to a decade working with a legal team preparing testimony for these various investigations and prosecutions, on top of my demanding day job and almost nightly speeches. It was certainly worth it when Luc was exonerated,* but there is no doubt that with this relentless total immersion in the genocide I couldn't have "moved on" even if I had wanted to.

At one point a superior of mine suggested that in light of all this, maybe I wanted to minimize my Rwanda presentations a bit. "After all," he said, "it is taking a lot of your time."

---

*   From the Belgian military court judge's summation: "The Court must note the legality of the order given on April 7, 1994, at 2:00 am by UNAMIR Commander General Dallaire to Kigali Sector Commander Colonel Marchal—to wit, to provide the Prime Minister with an escort. . . . We should also note that previously, General Dallaire and Colonel Marchal had attended, in part, a meeting that convinced them that the principal leaders of the Rwandan Armed Forces would continue their efforts toward the successful implementation of the Arusha Accord, while respecting the Rwandan constitution. . . . It was not up to the Accused [Luc Marchal] in any way to assess the need for or usefulness of executing the afore-mentioned order—the legal nature of which is not open to discussion—in achieving the greater good sought by the competent political authority. One thing is certain: the Accused was responsible for carrying out the order as given. Refusing to do so would have been unjustifiable."

From the UN's comment on the result of the court martial by Kofi Annan, Under-Secretary General for Peacekeeping Operations: "Given the international character of UNAMIR as a United Nations subsidiary organ, the operational control of the Secretary-General and his exclusive authority to issue orders and instructions within the limits of the mandate and through the chain of command, it is the view of the United Nations that Colonel Marchal acted within the mandate of the Force, in full compliance with the instructions of the United Nations Force Commander, and could not have acted otherwise without disobeying the Force Commander's instructions."

I suspected he was more worried about my ability to keep doing my job than about my well-being. But I knew I would not stop telling my story. I always managed to squeeze an hour here and another hour there from my day to keep making speeches. It was essential. Apart from my solemn promise to never let the world forget the genocide, those speeches were the *only* outlet I had. I was not going to give them up.

It was a very troubling time. I didn't sleep, I didn't laugh. I was alone.

In the midst of all this, I received a call from the chief of defence staff, Jean Boyle. He was a great guy, an officer who found it as hard as I did to play by unjust or outdated rules. In his usual unorthodox fashion, he arranged to meet me at a Swiss Chalet restaurant on Base Valcartier. We sat there, him in his brown leather pilot's jacket and me in my field green combat uniform, eating rotisserie chicken among the soldiers, as he confided in me his concerns about morale. We had worked together over many years, and he knew I valued being close to my troops and cared about their well-being as much as he did. There in that restaurant, surrounded by enlisted men and women, our shared concerns felt all the more real. He clearly recognized (in sharp contrast to the rest of the leadership) the impact of the past few years on the soldiers and their families.

He wanted me to come to Ottawa to take on the number two role in personnel; to look at the troops' quality of life and what was being done (or not being done) for them. This was a breath of fresh air in the ugly atmosphere that had developed between the troops and their leaders. His commitment was infectious, and even though I was only halfway through my current posting, his offer was intriguing. However, taking this new job would mean, for the first time in my career, being divorced from command. From cadets, through military college, to my first command and beyond, I had thrived on the mutual affection and loyalty that develops between commander and soldier, an almost paternalistic relationship, from which both benefit emotionally. This new position would separate me from the troops, but it would also be a great opportunity to influence policy on their behalf. And so I agreed to take on the job.

The family, once again, was not going to move with me. I would go to Ottawa on my own. This decision was hard on me, hard on us all, but I knew that raising the kids without me there five days out of seven was a sacrifice my wife was making to keep their lives stable, and I was grateful to her. It was my third posting in three years; it was selfish of me to expect them to uproot themselves every time I changed bases, especially since Beth knew first-hand (as I did) how hard life is for a soldier's child, always on the move, always having to make new friends. So, we agreed that she and the children would stay on in Quebec City, and I would go to Ottawa alone.

The atmosphere was still toxic when it came to "overprivileged" generals, so when the army clerk explained to me the choices of residence available in their Ottawa complex, he suggested I take one of the small one-bedroom apartments instead of the two-bedroom corner suites someone of my rank would have previously chosen, so as not to attract any negative attention. I didn't care one way or the other, and agreed.

Each floor of the complex had two-bedroom apartments that were roomy, bright corner units, and one-bedrooms that were about 300 square feet, stuck in the middle of the hallway. Mine was nasty, tiny and dark. On my first night in that dreary apartment—after a long day at work, a two-hour presentation on Rwanda, a supper of a cold can of creamed corn, and a few more hours of paperwork—I went into the tiny bedroom to try to sleep. I couldn't bring myself to shut the door. But even with it open, I was soon suffocating in the silence and the darkness of that little tomb. My senses, denied stimulation, gave my mind free rein.

As I tossed and turned, a jumble of memories fell over each other in the rush for attention, and my mind soon confused them into a half-sleeping, half-waking nightmare.

Standing at a roadblock, watching a machete crack a man's head in two.

Driving past women in pools of blood, broken bottles between their legs.

Crying babies, seeking their mothers.

Silent babies, lying on the ground.

Corpses forming a carpet of rags in all directions, the reds, yellows, and blues of what were once garments highlighting the stark white of exposed bone, the ashy grey of decomposing skin.

Taking turns walking in front of our vehicle, making sure we didn't run over any bodies, some of them only three-quarters dead. Others so horribly mutilated we couldn't pick them up whole.

A care package arriving from our wives: peanut butter, Cheez Whiz, chocolate, jujubes.

A little boy holding up his mangled stump where his hand had been beaten off with a club.

A creek filled with bloated bodies.

A bridge of bodies.

The suffocating smell. I can't breathe.

I am drowning in dark water, struggling to push my way up
    through the bodies. Gasping for air.
Breathing in blood.

I jerked to consciousness with a start, soaked in sweat, my heart racing. The clock read 11:55 p.m. Would the night never end? Stumbling into the kitchenette, I poured myself a drink and unwrapped a chocolate bar.

Over the next few days, I set up a replica of my office in that crummy little apartment. I didn't like staying late at work, and knew I wouldn't be able to get a good night's sleep in that horrible place, anyway. I never slept in the cell-like bedroom again, refusing to be a prisoner in that tiny space where all the spirits could invade. Instead, I nodded off at my desk, or on the small couch beside it. The lights were always on, keeping the darkness at bay.

I stayed there for almost a year. I worked twenty hours a day—on my official duties, on my speeches, and on the Letters Rogatory— only passing out each night when I'd exhausted myself.

The separation from direct command over my soldiers, plus the weight of the urgent responsibilities I now had for the welfare of all of the troops and their families, left me even more raw, more susceptible to the darkest of thoughts and memories. No one at work seemed to notice I was fraying—after all, I had just been moved into a high-profile job—but I knew something was changing, and it wasn't for the better. I had started to take small, unnecessary risks, like driving too fast (though never after drinking—I drew a firm line there).

For two years, work and adrenalin had warded off whatever was coming, but something inside me was now *demanding* attention, and it was using my dreams to make itself known, invading the little sleep I got. I dreamt of bodies moving through the water like fish, slimy against me. I was underwater, trying to get to the surface, but the closer I came, the thicker the bodies were. Many times I had a dream in which the souls of Rwandans surrounded me like jellyfish in a dark ocean. In another recurrent dream I was someplace very dark and a pair of eyes appeared, blinking like small lights. Then another pair, and another. More and more pairs of eyes. Some seemed angry, some were puzzled, and some were purely innocent. I knew these were the spirits of the slaughtered Rwandans.

The dream of eyes led me to another memory from the genocide: fifty, sixty, eighty thousand people walking in the cold rain, the red mud, with no protection from the weather, up and down the Rwandan hills. They filled the road completely, they were so tightly packed, and as they walked they dropped things that got heavy. The roads were filled with discarded stuff. And among these discards, in the rain, were elderly people too tired to go on. And children crying not only because they were hungry, and they were terribly hungry, but from fear.

I was in my vehicle, inching my way through these displaced tens of thousands, headed for a meeting to help negotiate a truce. Every now and again we had to stop because there was just no way to get through. At one such stop, I saw an old man propped against a tree. He was wet and he was exhausted and I could see that he was dying. I got out of the truck and he looked at me and our eyes locked. His were filled with bewilderment. How had it come to this? He had farmed his garden, raised his kids, survived other conflicts—and here he was dying alone in the mud.

On weekends not overtaken by my job or speaking events, I drove from Ottawa to Quebec City and back to visit the family, a 900-kilometre round trip. My Ottawa posting did not provide a driver, which was fine, though I missed the camaraderie with my old comrade, and I was concerned about losing so much productive worktime by having to drive myself. But I did not anticipate the effect that driving alone would have on me.

For the first time in years, I faced straight hours in which I had nothing to distract me. Hours in which I was alone with my thoughts. Alone with my feelings. Something about tearing down the highway at a hundred klicks in the absolute privacy of that little metal box unleashed deep emotions. For hours and hours, in the dark, a formless agony burst out of me—uncontrollable, racking. Oh, the things that went through my mind on those endless drives, as I blared music, stuffed myself with gas station junk food, smoked one cigar after another, screamed, cried, honked my horn. Christ, it was terrible.

I would arrive at the house, depleted, by midnight on Friday, and spend Saturday changing lightbulbs, scraping out eavestroughs, writing cheques, and scolding the children for offences committed through the week, watching them run off to their various activities. When I couldn't beg off, I'd do my best to get through the social engagements my wife had planned. Then after a rushed supper on Sunday, I'd find myself on the road again and wailing.

And so, living in that Ottawa hole-in-the-wall, all alone, attacked by the press and by my own mind, taking no nutrition, no sleep and no joy, I pushed the envelope hard for quality of life for the troops. It was an issue that desperately needed attention.

We clearly needed to rekindle our soldiers' pride in their work and encourage their willingness to serve. We needed to get out of the confrontational situation we had between the generals and the troops. And we really needed to handle the gap between a soldier's medical release and when Veterans Affairs Canada took over. Our people were falling between the cracks because there was no bridge. I knew the gap first-hand, from the experience of my driver back in Montreal. When I left for Ottawa, I'd made sure to tell my successor not to let him go back to an operational theatre. But he did, and the poor guy only lasted three months before he crashed. He's been trying to destroy himself ever since.

Soldiers were not only disgruntled by the lack of support they were getting when they came home, but many were so poorly paid they had to find second jobs to makes ends meet. Anecdotal evidence of troops returning from missions with psychological injuries was everywhere, yet we had no programmes established to deal with any of it. I wasn't the only one who saw that finding budget savings on the backs of soldiers while spending more on sending them into missions was an unsustainable burden on them, and that we had reached rock bottom in morale.

I threw myself into finding solutions. I set up a joint office with Veterans Affairs Canada and the Department of National Defence to ensure better coordination of services for returning troops. I arranged with Veterans Affairs to have a general officer seconded to them for more effective and better coordinated staffing of programmes and files. No less than our outgoing Judge Advocate General, Brigadier-General Pierre Boutet, was selected for the job and he remained there for nearly five years. Having someone of his rank inside Veterans Affairs was a great asset to both departments and to the modernization of the veteran support system.

I brought in legal experts and academics to propose reforms. I called on the help of David Hyman, a long-time colleague with the skills to consider this complex problem, and together we identified priority spending initiatives to improve quality of life to the tune of about five hundred million dollars a year, of which half was for salary increases alone. I began arguing within the Department of National Defence and the Canadian Forces about how badly we needed that new money. But any dollars the Forces had were going to the sharp end: sending and sustaining troops overseas. Since in polls the Canadian public gave national defence only a 15 percent approval rating, there were no votes to be scored by politicians if they spent on the military at all, let alone funding new initiatives.

I felt a growing indignation about working within a system that was clearly failing us all. And it had become very personal. I cared deeply about the welfare of the troops and their families, and was now carrying the full responsibility of resolving this crisis for them. My own family and I were experiencing the fallout of these cuts and the lack of concern for quality of life. Yet, because of my state of mind and my level of fatigue, I worried about whether I was the right person to do the job—whether I could sustain the pressures of fighting a system that seemed deaf to the needs of our most precious resources, the soldiers and their families. If I, as a two-star general, was not able to solve this, then what hopes did the junior ranks have?

Fighting for quality of life at this time was like fighting another war. And again, I felt like I was losing.

The beginning of the end occurred during a meeting of general officers with the interim chief of defence staff. He did not share the unorthodoxy and desire for reform of his predecessor. We were being briefed on more budget cuts when I found myself interrupting.

"I'm sorry, sir, but in the process of these budget cuts, quality of life is taking an awful shit-kicking." I doubt very much I used exactly those words, but this is certainly what I wanted to get across.

"On the contrary," came the reply from across the massive conference table. "Troops' quality of life has never been better. They are getting new equipment, they've got missions to accomplish, they are riding high, and keen!"

"Bullshit!" I exclaimed, and banged my fist on the table. Well, again, maybe that wasn't exactly how it came out, but I did demonstrate flagrant insubordination. That afternoon, I received a note requesting me to be at the CDS's office the next morning.

I arrived as ordered and sat down before him. He explained to me that the concerns I had for the soldiers and for their families were exaggerated. "We have Veterans Affairs taking care of things and we are doing our best.

"You are obviously under stress," he said gently, but firmly. "Perhaps you should get some help."

He was the first person in the chain of command to notice — or at least the first to tell me to my face. He was also my superior, and so I was obliged to obey.

I made my way to the National Defence Medical Centre, where I was assigned to receive group therapy with six other wounded military personnel. It was an all-ranks group; some had been in theatres of operations and some had suffered trauma from sexual harassment or car accidents. I was a two-star general who had been responsible for the lives of hundreds of soldiers and millions of civilians during the worst mass atrocity we had seen since the Shoah, and yet I was being encouraged to share that trauma with this group under the guidance of a young therapist I wasn't sure could even spell Rwanda. I'm not denigrating the wisdom of the group, or the reality of what any of them had been through and were struggling with. But it just didn't make any sense at all for me to talk to them about what I was going through, or even the world I came from; there just wasn't enough shared knowledge, and there was too much to explain. I did one session, and that was it. I didn't go back.

Instead, I had to undergo weekly one-on-one sessions with the same novice therapist, who was on a steep learning curve, still trying to comprehend the operational culture, to learn the terminology of the army and the realities of war. She started pumping me full of pills that didn't work and gave me all kinds of nasty side effects (everything from dizziness and dry mouth to confusion and forgetfulness). To my mind, these sessions didn't do anything except create a hell of a lot of anxiety, by pushing me to relive the war. The sessions, combined with the pills that made me unsure of how I was feeling, made for a terrible disorientation. My moods swung wildly and my nightmares became more and more vivid.

When I reported this to the therapist, she said I was likely suffering from sleep deprivation and sent me for an all-night test for sleep apnea. Of course, the results were "inconclusive," because the problem lay not in my airway, but in the corridors of my mind.

That winter, during one my six-hour drives to see the family in Quebec City, I had my first concrete experience with how far I was falling. I was on the highway in a wretched state. Approaching an overpass, I realized I could simply wrench the wheel to the left, and smash into the support column in the middle of the lanes. The thought was so sudden, and so clear.

I swerved the car, hard, and sped toward the concrete column.

But there was a huge pile of plowed snow at the sides and in the median of the highway. Instead of crashing into the column, the car bounced off the snowbank and back onto the road. Immediately, my suicidal trance was broken, and I regained control of the car.

From that moment, I knew suicide was a reality for me.

—

WAITING FOR FIRST LIGHT 69

At work, I was still getting nowhere on quality of life. I took the raw data I had accumulated on the condition of the troops and their morale, and reached out to different branches of the National Defence headquarters in order to muster support and funds. No luck.

Then I had the idea of approaching the parliamentary committee on defence and veterans' affairs in the House of Commons, to find out what they were doing about the issue, or if it was even on their radar. But I couldn't go to the committee directly and ask: I was supposed to make a request to our policy people, which they would forward to the minister of defence, whose office would pass it on to the committee, which would then consider whether to respond. It seemed ridiculous, and from my previous experiences inside the Defence Department, I figured that it would not work. So I decided to jump the line.

I went directly to Parliament Hill to see a member of the committee. Of course, it was totally prohibited for me to approach any politician on a fundamental policy point in this way, and I had absolutely no authority or right to do so. Yet my time in Rwanda, when I had been dealing directly with heads of government, had stripped away my patience for the way "things are done." I'd had enough—the vets and their families had had enough. So I brazenly showed up at this politician's office in the Confederation Building, in uniform, to discuss it.

He had been a brigadier-general in the Reserves, and it turned out, he was willing to talk with me. I explained the situation, and the need for tangible evidence that would force National Defence and the government to address the problem. I recommended an urgent, in-depth, cross-country study and analysis of our soldiers' quality of life.

As I left his office, I didn't know what would come of it, but I was glad I had taken this step. In a senior management meeting two days later, the interim chief of defence staff briefed us: "I don't know who got to the minister," he said, "but it seems that they are doing a major quality of life study over the next twelve months."

The study's findings supported my original recommendations, and at the end of it we received close to five hundred million dollars in new funding for quality of life initiatives, including an 18 percent pay increase for Canadian Forces members. It was a bright spot in a dark time.

At that time in the military, when you were sent to a new posting you were allowed to be separated from your family for a year, but then they were supposed to join you. If the family decided not to, they were no longer permitted to rent military quarters, and your separated-family allowances were stopped. I'd now spent almost a year in Ottawa, and if Beth and the children didn't soon come to join me, they'd have to leave their military lodgings, and we'd have to buy or rent elsewhere.

I told Beth one weekend that I had been to see some houses in the Ottawa area, in Gatineau and in the pretty town of Aylmer. We had lived there at one time, so we knew it and had friends there, too. But no, she did not want to live anywhere near Ottawa, where she perceived we would be under the scrutiny all generals were subjected to at the time.

I liked Quebec City, the whole romantic dimension of it, and I was fine with thinking of it as a place where I might one day retire. Now was not the right time, but Beth insisted on staying. So I told her to find a house there, and told the army that I was moving out of that dreadful apartment into a new place of my own in the Ottawa area.

—

I found a small but bright place in Gatineau, just across the short bridge that separates Ontario from Quebec. I could see the Parliament Buildings on the other shore from my window, and I was only a ten-minute drive from the office in Ottawa, but it afforded me a certain pleasant distance from the public eye. The Ottawa River acts as more than a border between French and English Canada; it is also a major psychological barrier. On the Quebec side, I felt safe from the politics and the media that were plaguing me—not to mention the threats made against me by some extremists who had come here from Rwanda. During the genocide, Rwandan radio had put a target on me and, apparently, there was still a contract out on my head.

The new apartment was a major improvement, but it did not come without stress. This new situation of two residences and no subsidization was going to cost me an additional $30,000 a year. I still had to make the long drive to Quebec City each weekend. And I was still alone.

To be fair, I never put my foot down and insisted they had to join me. I did not willingly abandon my family, but in some ways it suited me to be apart from them. During the day, when I was in my stable state, I'd feel disappointed they weren't with me. But when I was in my darker, night-time world, I was kind of glad they weren't around. I'm not proud of that; at the time I didn't even understand it. All I knew was that whenever I didn't have to be in public, I would avoid social interaction at all costs. I sought isolation deliberately, but also somehow unconsciously. I craved affection, but I couldn't bear to be around anyone—family or friends—who could give it.

Also, by agreeing to what became a permanent living arrangement, I was tacitly agreeing that they needed protection from me. On weekends with them, I'd sometimes hear myself shouting at my wife or yelling at the kids. My little son would ask for a toy, or my daughter would refuse to eat something on her plate, and I would bark at them, "Do you realize? Do you have any idea what other children . . ." Then I would proceed to describe some horror to them, until they were in tears. I watched myself doing it, telling myself to stop as my anger and aggression and righteous indignation escalated. I never hit them, like my father hit me, but I sure as hell scared them. I simply could not control what came out of my mouth, what my eyes saw, how my body was moving. I was conscious of what I was doing; I just couldn't stop it.

There was no getting better, because there was no moving on. I couldn't move on, because the horrors moved with me. Every night, if I slept, I lived it again. Every day, if I turned on the news, I lived it again.

On weekends, I would see the family watching TV news, and they would seem to me unfathomable in their ability to sit in a chair and watch horrors unfold in front of them. Of course, it was unreasonable of me, even crazy, but that was how it truly seemed to my troubled mind, because those people and places ravaged by violence that were flashing up on the screen were as real to me as if they had been standing, bleeding and crying, in our living room. I was envious of others' ability to insulate themselves from these horrors.

When you are living a war—its extremes of noise and smells and chaos, the faces of the human beings in every state of life and death and fear and pain—you cannot get away from it. For me, the war did not become the past. It was not history. It was, and is, alive in my mind and my being with nearly the intensity of the day it happened.

Before Rwanda, when I used to watch the news, I took it in as information, like everyone else. Now, I sensed it. I actually felt the heat from the burning houses, I saw the child soldiers, I heard the gunfire and the refugees' screams of anguish, I smelled the smoke and the killing. To me it was *reality*. I was back in it, reliving the war and the genocide. I knew I was not actually at risk, but it seemed so present. Kind of like my nightmares: they may not have been real, but they were the truth.

That is what makes it so difficult when people ask you to move on: "You've been back five years. Ten years. Twenty years. Get over it." The problem is that you simply can't do it, because it *just* happened. Just now. Either in flashbacks or in dreams. And so you try to blot it out by any means: medication and therapy, drugs and alcohol, whatever will throw you off this playing field of horror.

Back in Ottawa, I would work maniacally all day, then drive who-knows-where to make a presentation on the genocide, then head to my new apartment where I had once again set up a replica of my office. There I would go on working until my head dropped. Or, more and more frequently, I would go down to the park in front of my building, which bordered the river, and sit on a bench. I'd just sit there for hours, in the middle of the night, freezing, looking out over the water. Sometimes I'd stand and gaze down into it. And sometimes I even waded in, willing the frigid water to slip over me.

Inevitably, the minute that the first grey signs of daybreak showed in the sky, or a bird started to sing, I would come out of my daze. It was weird; I would realize a new day was coming, and make my way with haste to my apartment. I was finally able to sleep just as the sun began to rise. In the summer months, this would give me three or four hours of rest before I'd have to go to the office. In winter, I'd have to be at work before the sun was up, and rest was almost impossible.

One of my wife's sisters, Christine, also lived in Gatineau, and over time she became very helpful to me. She, her daughter, and a niece who was living with them all kept an eye on me. My sister-in-law would come by on occasion for supper, and we would talk. Or one of the girls would hang out and watch TV on the sofa, just to be near. Beth was grateful that they were looking out for me. They knew I was not well. And at last so did I.

Then, over the course of a few short weeks, we were hit with several suicides among troops who had been to Yugoslavia and Rwanda (though none who served during my time as force commander; these were soldiers who had deployed after I left). It seemed that every few days there was another report of a soldier who had taken his own life, and the media began asking how the Canadian Forces were addressing this problem.

Since the Forces' medical system was under personnel's area of responsibility, it was up to us to respond. Because I'd been in one of these complex missions, and I was a two-star general who spoke both English and French, and I was the number two in personnel, I was elected to meet with the media and explain our position.

I received a briefing package from the medical and legal branches, laying out the official line and talking points. I read it, aghast: it stated unequivocally that these suicides were *not* a result of deployments. It said that if soldiers were killing themselves, it was not the mission that was the catalyst, but their own psychological instability. A predisposition to suicide, combined with pre-existing personal difficulties (family problems, financial troubles), made the mission, at most, a possible contributing factor in the much larger picture of the crises that triggered their deaths. The briefing documents went on to say that regardless of the cause, it was impossible to prevent all suicides, and our average was no worse than the general population's.

I found the thought of standing up in public and saying any of this unimaginable.

Since 1991, we had stumbled unprepared into a series of missions in places in the world where we had never expected to deploy — Iraq, Kuwait, Cambodia, Yugoslavia, Somalia, Rwanda — each with racial, ethnic and religious complexities we had no concept of. Our troops had witnessed — were still witnessing — previously unimagined, massive abuses of human rights, and extraordinary deprivation and depravity. They were facing for the first time the shocking ruthlessness of belligerents with no respect for the rule of law, or rules of armed conflict, in imploding nations and those caught in civil wars. We'd been deploying thousands of troops into these mission areas over the past few years, and we were rotating them every six months. This meant that we had soldiers who had been on three or more very demanding missions over a period of only five or six years.

We had trained them for none of it. The classic peacekeeping operations we'd previously engaged in did not resemble anything we were ad hocing our way through now, and our troops were forced to learn on the job. From the general right down to the private, we were often facing ethical, moral and legal dilemmas for which we were entirely unprepared: from imposed non-intervention when women were being raped and killed, to witnessing mass slaughter, to facing armed children.

My staff at personnel and I were still having arguments with the legal and medical branches of the Canadian Forces about the reality of "Gulf War syndrome." There was no agreement on whether we should be helping troops, financially and otherwise, for an injury that no one understood. Yet we were making more and more demands on them to be deployable, thus putting more and more pressure on them and their families to maintain some kind of normalcy.

Psychological injuries were a new phenomenon to us, despite what history should have taught us. We didn't have the terms sorted out, we didn't really understand how it happened, we weren't too sure what all the symptoms and impacts were. But we did know that some of our guys (especially those among the junior ranks, young and unprepared, who were the ones sent into villages and who encountered mutilated bodies) were ending up unable to function. They had become an administrative problem—drunks and drug users, undisciplined and ineffective. Until now we'd been dealing with these casualties by either throwing them out of the Forces or hiding them within the system and hoping they'd get better. But now that a number of suicides in rapid succession had caught the attention of the media, we had to take a stand. And the stand they were telling me to take was one of denial.

A press conference was scheduled. I brooded over it for days. I was well aware the troops and their families were under severe stress. I had begun to recognize these stresses in myself and my own family. I certainly didn't believe I had any predisposition to mental illness or to suicidal thoughts; on the contrary, before Rwanda, I had always been quite light-hearted, always the one to find the fun, crack a joke, or plan a party. The army was everything I knew and everything I loved, and my work had been at the core of my joie de vivre. I lost all that joy, as a direct result of the genocide. I suspected that our lawyers and medical people had put together this briefing as a pre-emptive defence against the lawsuits and pension or compensation claims that would come our way if it was ever proven that people had been psychologically injured in operational theatres, or had died of those injuries.

More and more, this was how I was seeing wounds like mine: as potentially terminal injuries. And yet I was expected to present a mealymouthed, institution-protecting explanation for military suicides to the public.

Instead, I turned it upside down.

I showed up at the press conference, which was being held in the auditorium of our National Defence Medical Centre, and I told the national press that I did *not* believe that these men would have committed suicide without the impact of the mission. I said that we needed to conduct major reforms in our care of this injury. I told them that in order to implement the politically mandated budget cuts, the Canadian Forces had cut our medical staff by at least half at a time when we needed *more* medical professionals, not fewer, in order to deal with this potentially deadly injury.

I also revealed that I, too, was a casualty.

My announcement didn't get much airplay, nor did anyone in the leadership address it with me directly. But afterward, Stéphane Grenier, a young public affairs officer who had deployed to Rwanda, got in touch with me and a few others who had been there, and with the support of our new CDS, General Maurice Baril (who had been my UN Department of Peacekeeping Operations boss when I was in Rwanda), we filmed a short internal video.

Together, we were going to force the system to recognize this injury and deal with it, and encourage others to come forward. Called *Witness the Evil*, the video was the first formal educational and informational tool about these new conflicts, and the intrusive and complex injuries—specifically, post-traumatic stress disorder, PTSD—that can result from them. It interspersed raw footage of the Rwandan massacre with details about the Canadian mission there and interviews with Canadians who had served.

They all told their personal stories with solid professionalism, wearing full uniform. Still, a few uncontrollable tears welled in the eyes of these battle-hardened veterans as they shared some of the unthinkable things they had experienced.

"We went into a school," remembered one blue beret, the camera tight on his face. "They had all the children lined up, and it looked like they played a game with the children. Like, they . . . they . . ." Here he faltered for a beat then carried on. "They chopped their heads off, and then they'd sign their names." His voice cracked as he said to someone off-camera, "No, I'm okay. I've got to get this out." He continued, "And I think, 'How can people do this?' I wasn't accustomed to this. I'd done my sentry duties, and I'd been out in the field, but . . . I don't know."

Another young man recalled stepping off a path to relieve himself in the bushes. "I step over a bump and my foot sinks straight down. I hear all this snapping like twigs. I look down to pull my foot out of the mud and see I was in the chest cavity of a body. So instead of doing the normal thing and taking one step back, I kind of leapt backwards and tripped and rolled into a mass grave." Simply, stoically, he admitted, "I kind of had a freak-out episode, so I scrambled out of there as soon as I could."

The last few minutes of the video announced the Department of National Defence's new strategies to address post-traumatic stress disorder. "PTSD is an ailment soldiers who've served in difficult environments such as Bosnia, Somalia and Rwanda may develop," recited the narrator. "It is a physical condition in which the chemical signals of the brain change, which can affect a soldier's behaviour in theatre and once back home. While doctors are optimistic that treatment programmes can relieve many of the symptoms, much about the disorder is still unknown, and it can take years for the symptoms of PTSD to be felt and recognized."

The voice-over then spelled it out: "Many were left feeling alone. For them, asking for help meant being labelled as weak, or cowardly. A label that could eat away at a promising military career. So they bottled up the sights, the sounds, the smells, and the pain and locked them away. But the horror never really disappears, and months or years later, the trauma bubbles to the surface."

Next, the peacekeepers' faces reappeared on the screen, this time visibly shaken. One said, "It's nothing what I expected. I expected to do my job, as a medic, and just carry on. But you couldn't just carry on. It affected me, it affected my wife. It was hard."

These young men and women spelled out everything I had been holding in. One of them said, "That's one of the hardest things about being a Canadian soldier, is that weakness is frowned upon, so the easiest thing to do is to take everything and push it aside and pretend it was a movie. And it isn't until you get hit by smells—the smells are the worst—that will trigger a memory, and it's like a film starting up in your head. There are foods I can't eat anymore. Grilled chicken. Can't eat it. Looks like a dead body. Rusted-out vehicles, can't go near them. Children . . . I have a hell of a time looking at them, especially newborns, because they were a plaything for the Hutu extremists." Tears rolled down the soldier's face as he croaked out, "They really liked killing kids."

And then it was my turn: a general, a commander, making an unheard-of confession. "I don't shout it from the rooftops, but I've . . . I have undergone ten months of therapy. It didn't hit me right away, it took nearly two years to all of a sudden not be able to cope. Not being able to forget it or keep it in the drawer. And," I continued, the muscles in my face visibly contorting against the words I was forcing myself to say, "I became suicidal. Because there was no other solution. You couldn't live with the pain and the sounds and the smell and the sights. I couldn't sleep. I couldn't stand the loudness of silence. Sometimes I wished I'd lost a leg, instead of having those grey cells screwed up. You lose a leg, it's obvious, and you get your treatment. You lose your marbles, it is difficult to explain, difficult to gain that support that you need. But those who don't recognize it are going to be a risk to themselves and to us."

And finally, General Baril appeared on the screen, assuring the viewer: "Not everyone who has witnessed such horror will develop post-traumatic stress disorder. But those who do suffer from stress-related ailments are fully entitled to, and deserve, the help they need to get back to their normal life." Baril unequivocally stated, "PTSD is nothing to be ashamed of. Like so many other medical conditions, it can be treated."

Mostly the video was greeted with uncomfortable silence from my colleagues in the leadership of the Canadian Forces. I think they thought my participation in it was inappropriate, and that I was nuts for showing my vulnerability. But the response from the troops was very positive. Almost immediately, NCOs began approaching me, thanking me for coming forward. Time and again, they would share their painful, personal stories with me, right there on the pavement, in hallways or in elevators. Even in the can. It was remarkable, and terribly sad.

Emboldened by the categorical support expressed in the video, and by the troops who clearly agreed that *enough was enough*, I travelled to Vermont to meet with the head of the U.S. Department of Veterans Affairs' National Center for PTSD. The American experience with casualties from the Vietnam War put them years ahead of us in treatment and in making the system work for veterans with this injury. I decided I'd had it with half-assed, useless therapy—not just for me, but for the entire Forces. I told the doctor that I needed his help to build a mental health support system to take care of our injured. I ended our meeting by saying that I thought maybe I needed some help, too.

He was a practising psychiatrist, and agreed to take me on as a patient. I started going down to Vermont every six weeks to see him. Beth or one of my staff would drive me there and back—I couldn't risk such a long drive on my own. I felt that we were on the right track immediately, but these sessions were very hard, very demanding. I'd leave them, having talked for two hours solid, feeling worse than when I went in. This routine was reinforced by regular meetings with a psychologist in Ottawa. Therapy was pulling everything to the surface, and that was awful. Of course, I wasn't doing it to feel good; it was more like taking your medicine, hoping you'd get better as a result.

Treatment for PTSD was all so new, for everyone, and it wasn't perfect by a long shot. I would leave my sessions feeling desperately alone, with nowhere to put the emotions that had been churned up. I felt I was locked into a bubble of horror, and the outside world just didn't exist anymore. I wasn't living, only reliving.

The endless experimentation with medication was also brutal. The doctors were constantly changing the pills or the dose, trying to find a balance that minimized side effects, and gave me some reasonable control on my daytime emotions, as well as the night horrors.

I noticed more and more professionals were discussing the value of injured veterans having an animal. Even my boss, Maurice, claimed that without his dog he never would have survived coming off the missions he did. I felt I desperately needed the presence of another living creature in my life; something warm and welcoming—who would simply sit by me and listen. Something innocent and fragile that I could offer protection to, having failed to protect so many. So I went out and got a bird. A canary. There it was in its cage, just being alive. I would sit and watch it as it bounced around. It was safe and it was fed, and it gave me a semblance of serenity. But, of course, an animal requires consistent care, and cleaning, and company, too—more than I could handle given the pace I was working and how little I was at home. I had the bird for only a couple of months, before I reluctantly found it a better place to live.

So, the hollow loneliness remained in me. The medication, the therapy, new and ongoing hassles at work and internationally: I couldn't take it all alone. Thank God for my sister-in-law. After my therapy sessions I often reached out to Christine. She lived reasonably close by, and she always came when I called. She would come to my apartment and she would sit and listen to me rant for hours at a time. She never interrupted. Never asked for a clarification, or a description, just listened as I ran the gamut of emotions. She provided me with the missing, and *essential*, part of my treatment: peer support.

By the end of those hours, she'd still be the rock I needed. I'd be sweating and fatigued from walking in circles and talking and shouting, and at last I would find myself empty. Completely drained, and even wanting sleep. I can never thank her enough for her patience, her generosity, her humanity and her courage.

I was up for a promotion to three-star general, and the job of assistant deputy minister, human resources (military). I figured the senior leadership was having second thoughts after my PTSD revelation, but I was determined to get the promotion, not because I was interested in the improved rank but because I thought that in this position I'd really be able to change things for the better.

Thankfully, the assessment my psychologist supplied to the CDS was very positive, stating that "the majority of the presenting symptoms have disappeared, and [have been] replaced with feeling of serenity." I don't remember intentionally misleading her, but I did know the promotion boards were sitting. So I likely put my best foot forward during our sessions, knowing if I was diagnosed with active PTSD I would never be promoted. And though the sessions had been difficult, I think I was optimistic that the therapy might actually have done the trick.

I got the star and the job. I now had a hundred thousand military and civilian Canadian Forces and DND personnel under my jurisdiction. The workload increased, but that was fine with me. The more work there was, the easier it was to drown out my injury.

Around this time, I received a small piece of good news. The blue-ribbon Carnegie Commission on Preventing Deadly Violence, which had been investigating the Rwandan genocide, published a report that vindicated me, stating that if I had been given a well-equipped and well-trained force of as few as five thousand soldiers in early 1994, we would have averted the slaughter of half a million people.

Through the months and years of being publicly challenged, even in some quarters vilified, not to mention my endless nights digging through documents and my memory to satisfy various inquiries, and innumerable other nights questioning myself and every split-second decision I made in the midst of the genocide, this was the first overt expression of public support I'd received, and I welcomed it.

But the biggest trial was still to come.

In 1998, I made my first trip to Arusha, Tanzania, to testify at the International Criminal Tribunal for Rwanda—the court established by the UN to try those accused of being responsible for the genocide. At this point, the tribunal had not yet received any testimony as to the way the genocide had unfolded. They had heard eyewitness accounts of specific events from individuals, but they didn't have the whole picture of what all parties were doing: the Rwandan government, the rebel forces, my mission, and the UN. My responsibility would be to give the court an overview of the war—how it started, how it was implemented and how it ended—as well an account of my command, my mission and the decisions I'd taken that had affected the lives of so many. The preparation once again meant going through my daytimers day by day so I could walk the court through every detail. It felt like commanding the mission a second time.

But this was about more than relating events—I would be cross-examined, too. Unlike the Letters Rogatory for the Belgian investigation, I would face questions in person. I would also be the most senior person testifying; whatever I said would have a significant impact on all the other testimony regarding the mission.

UN peacekeeping force commanders had never gone in front of such a tribunal before, either to present information for the prosecution or to be cross-examined by defence; the UN was on new ground. I was concerned about setting a precedent for other force commanders, but also, of course, about having defence lawyers conduct an examination of my actions in the field. And there is the special challenge of explaining military decisions to civilians who have never experienced war.

While I remembered the facts and I remembered the actions, the paperwork from the mission did not describe every single solitary thing that happened. I had kept notes diligently, but in some cases only had my memory to rely on. I was terribly, terribly troubled by concerns that I would fail to provide the right information. I knew that I was not functioning as effectively as I could, suffering as I was from PTSD. By definition of that injury, I was not a person who could easily handle stress; I was instead someone who could be easily confused under stress. I wanted to ensure that justice was done, but I was having doubts about my ability to keep it together between the ears.

And so, the preparations were gruelling. Once again I methodically read and reread documents in order to grasp everything that had happened and explain my decision-making processes at the time. My own legal counsel put me through extensive cross-examination to prepare me for whatever questions might come at me. The entire exercise was painful and unpleasant.

Several times, over the weeks before I left for Arusha, I went to the nearby cathedral over the lunch hour to sit quietly in a pew. The serenity of the building and the odour of incense from a thousand masses reminded me of another dimension to life, a tradition I had been raised in but that I was having difficulty adhering to now. I sat at the back of the church, tears pouring down my cheeks, asking myself why I was doing all this.

I didn't have to testify; it was totally voluntary. In fact, the UN and the Canadian government would have been much happier if I had refused. The doctors were against my doing it; there was no doubt in their minds this effort was inflaming the wound. Colleagues and family told me not to do it. Some were worried about my mental and physical safety in Africa; others insisted I had already done my part. For years I'd been doing everything I could to block the pain and the anguish. Why was I volunteering to dive deeper into it?

Not testifying was never a possibility for me. I had an automatic answer to any request concerning the genocide: *Yes.* I was pushed by a driving force that overrode logic, the demands of my health, even my fears that I'd fail again. It kept pushing me forward, but I did not understand it.

A team of eight joint task force members accompanied me to Arusha, along with Brent and my legal counsel. The JTF was the elite commando unit of the Canadian military, and all eight soldiers were on hand to keep me safe. They even travelled with litres of blood in my type, so sure were they of the risk I was running.

I couldn't help but reflect on being surrounded by all this capability in a country that was at peace, just because there might be an attempt on my life in order to prevent me from testifying, and yet when I'd needed resources and support to protect hundreds of thousands of civilians in Rwanda, I had next to nothing. It just wasn't right.

The trial commenced, and my testimony went smoothly. Despite the defence coming at me with a revisionist, conspiratorial line of questioning, on cross-examination I kept my answers clear, concise and, I think, helpful.

One unexpected, and demoralizing, dimension of my partici-pation in the tribunal was that, after this further intense round of scrutiny of my mission, I began to question my own under-standing of what had happened. Had I been duped during the genocide? I left Arusha thinking back over all my attempts at negotiation between the Rwandan interim government and the Rwandan Patriotic Front. I wondered to what extent I had been a patsy in the middle of these adversaries. This realization caused a deeply distressing new doubt in me that served to undermine the purpose of my being there in the first place.

Two days after I returned from Arusha I had a therapy session in Vermont with my psychiatrist. About two and a half hours in, I started to have incredible chest pains. It felt like a heart attack, and the doctor sure as shit thought it was one, so called an ambulance.

On the gurney being rushed through the emergency room, I was furious I was going to die in hospital and not in the field. But they stabilized me, and conducted tests to establish what had caused the episode.

Finally, the doctors told me it hadn't been a heart attack. There was nothing wrong with any of my organs. In effect, the attack had been caused by my metabolism closing down. My brain had become so fatigued that it would not allow my body to continue to function and my body had almost quit.

A perverse idea took root in me. What if I could force a per-manent shutdown? If I could push my body and brain past their limits, there would be no more torment.

I'd spent years trying to drown the pain with work, with speeches, with food. These had been attempts to avoid or neu-tralize the memories. But now I wondered if the opposite method of dealing with them would be more effective: instead of trying to dull myself into oblivion by relentless diversionary tactics, what if I tried to recreate those extraordinarily powerful, fear- and adrenalin-driven emotions that I'd experienced in Rwanda? If testifying at the tribunal had elicited a near-shutdown, I reckoned that I could accomplish a final, total breakdown and brain collapse by somehow immersing myself in the incredible horrors that I experienced.

If I could do that then I might just finally crash.

I recalled a professor I had heard speak at a British higher command staff course I took in 1991, at the height of the Gulf War. He'd theorized that soldiers receive more powerful stimulation from combat than from sexual climax, because in combat at any moment you could die. And all around you are extraordinary sensory stimuli — explosions, violence, death — that put your body on the highest alert and cause it to perceive at the highest pitch.

He said that it was common for soldiers to seek that high again, because they had lived it and survived it; although it wasn't enjoyable, it was extreme and it was addictive. In response, some take on more missions. They keep going back, shipping out within months of returning. They are operationally keen, of course, but in some cases they are being psychologically pulled, too.

That wasn't really an option for me. I was so wrapped up in the tasks I was doing, there was no room for me to take on another mission. So where else could I find a replication of the scale and intensity of what I witnessed?

When the goal is to destroy an entire group of people, achieving total annihilation by murdering every last person can prove difficult. But instilling terror in a population will go a long way toward successfully destroying them by destroying their will to live.

Killing children in front of parents, killing parents in front of children, forcing children to kill parents in order to save siblings, inflicting vicious injury to force the living to witness the pain and suffering of the dying: these were just some of the atrocities committed by the extremists during the genocide in Rwanda.

Often victims were intentionally left alive, to suffer and spread fear. We witnessed innumerable people left alive with their extremities cut off, or with machete wounds down to the bone. People hacked and tossed alive into latrines to drown in filth, with others forced to stand and watch, so they lived the suffering before it happened to them or to their children.

These tactics were hideous and inhuman, and this was exactly the point: to dehumanize the "enemy" and make their suffering no different than a fly whose wings have been plucked off.

But there was a further depraved common element pervading the brutality, which only truly registered in my mind many months after I came home from the mission. With all I had witnessed, at the time and in the thick of it, I somehow hadn't been able to make sense of what was in front of me.

It hadn't been enough to mutilate them. Now I saw it clearly: victims had been sexually abused and degraded in their last moments. Those had not been random body parts we'd seen, but sexual organs, chopped off and piled, or stuffed into the mouths of corpses.

Now, it seemed like every time I shut my eyes, I saw those images clearly. Women split open from the vagina to the sternum. Men with their genitals chopped off, or their buttocks, left to bleed to death. The *génocidaires* had used rape as a weapon as ruthlessly as the machete. Rape of women, boys, and girls. This horrific, intentional degradation now stood out in memory more vividly than it had in the fog of war: bodies left totally or nearly naked, sexual organs mutilated or with painful insertions; young boys forced to rape their mothers after a promise to spare them, then clearly murdered in mid-act, their bodies left intact to tell the tale to all survivors.

Sexual violence had not been the exception, and it had not been spontaneous. Broadcasts over the radio had incited rape as a highly effective tool in the genocide; the minister of youth had even incited her own sons to commit this act of degradation as a means to achieve the end of the Tutsi ethnic group by destroying their targets' humanity.

This extreme horror had finally made itself known to me, burrowing up from whatever part of my brain in which I'd hidden it. It invaded me, and I could not get away from it. It was there, inside me, every time I closed my eyes. I didn't have to find a way to replicate the horror: I carried these indelible images inside me.

In the aftermath of my physical collapse, I let down all the feeble barriers I'd erected: I *wanted* the horror to crash my brain, like tilting a pinball machine, causing a complete shutdown. Night after night I would dwell on these horrors, purposefully playing them out in my head, trying to find ways to replicate the hideous intensity of those memories. Being witness to such extreme sexual violence as we see in theatres of operation often and naturally leads many veterans to seek out violence, abuse, self-harm, sex addiction or pornography, as well as the old standbys of booze, drugs and courting danger in a hundred different ways. Over the years, during my darkest, tormented nights, I experimented with many of these in hopes of pushing my mind beyond its limits. I sought self-destruction, to lobotomize myself, to become a vegetable, because a vegetable can't hurt.

I never succeeded, though. The result was simply more guilt, more shame.

The nights felt endless. Though finally, the birds would start singing outside, and I would at last allow the torment to cease for another day.

At the same time as I was using my nights to try to torture myself into a permanent collapse, in the daylight I was urgently pushing to influence the medical branch of the Canadian Forces, which was now under my command, to change its attitude toward mental health and build up its capacity to deal with it. I began to share some of the information from the PTSD Center in the United States, as well as their example of how to build a more effective system.

Through our work to bring a better understanding of PTSD to the Canadian Forces, I came to realize that I was not *nuts*. We coined the term operational stress injury (OSI), and in this way we were able to argue that our people (myself, included) were suffering from injuries that needed to be treated just like the wounds you could see. We aimed to promote the same sense of urgency in treating people with operational stress injuries as we had for physical injuries, because every day someone lives with an untreated OSI is another day that it gets worse. This shift in terminology and attitude was helpful in securing therapy, and dealing with stigma, but it did not mean all would be well in a week. PTSD required long-term treatment, and it was not going to be easy for anyone.

Despite this work, I was getting worse. Sometimes I would have difficult therapy sessions that reawakened new memories; sometimes the pills screwed me up. Increasingly, I found that I had little tolerance for criticism. I experienced impatience with everything, from home to work. I was always fighting to control my rage. My wife would accuse me of flying off the handle at any little comment of hers. I was surprised to hear this, as I felt I was constantly holding back. My reactions weren't half as extreme as they could have been, and I knew that neither of us would want to hear what I would say if I really let go. I could see that I was scaring my family, that I was overreacting, but I just couldn't stop. After all I'd witnessed, shouting—any amount of shouting— didn't seem so bad. Which was the injury talking and not the man I used to be.

Emotional extremes would happen when I was alone, too. Like the fits of rage, fits of anguish would overtake me. As always, I was travelling a lot, giving my presentations on Rwanda and, as my profile had risen, I was asked to speak farther and farther afield. I often had to stay in a hotel after an event and drive or fly back to Ottawa for work the next morning. Alone on the road, alone in hotel rooms, sitting on the bed, staring at the four walls, I would be overcome. A noise or a smell, or even just the spiral of fatigue combined with the content of my speech, would trigger anguish. My soul was feeling such acute sadness and despair that these emotions would completely take over my body, leaving me fearful and with a constant feeling of vulnerability. I didn't know what the exact triggers were, so I never knew what would set me off. In the eyes of the world, it seemed I was still functioning normally. I was showing up for work, and working hard. I was giving presentations. I was going home on weekends to be with my family. But I was haunted: what if I lost it for real?

My fear of myself and my reactions led me to avoid even more rigorously all non-essential encounters with people, and I even started to dread the essential ones. I would see work events in my calendar—mess dinners, meetings, anything where I would be interacting with others—and just seeing them in ink would give me a hollow anxiety.

Beth and I had once been a very sociable couple; it was part and parcel of regimental life, and we had both enjoyed it. Now I cancelled everything, further isolating myself and Beth, too. I felt I couldn't risk entering an environment where I might be unable to keep up a facade of calm; what if I exploded because of something somebody said, or because of a sound, or a smell, or a visual cue? Constant dread ate away at me; I never felt any peace; I never felt secure. I was always looking over my shoulder, never sure to what extent I would react or how far I would go.

I did occasionally open up about all this with my closest colleague and boss, Maurice. He had been deeply affected by our experiences in Rwanda, too, but he dealt with it differently: where I dived into the depths, he had simply locked the hatch. But that didn't mean he didn't fully understand. He did. Over the years we had become quite close, and he kept a careful watch over me.

A fellow combat arms officer, he loved to refurbish old rifles. I, too, had a few rifles, presents and hand-me-downs from my father and father-in-law. When we were talking informally one day, Maurice suggested that maybe I wanted to think about not keeping those guns in the house. He had a lovely big lock-up in his home, and offered to hold on to them for me. I asked my doctors about it, and they strongly recommended that I hand them over to him for safekeeping. He still has them.

Around this time, I also noticed I was having problems driving. I would be at a street corner, waiting for the light, and when it turned green, I'd panic because I didn't know where I was. It didn't matter that I'd driven that route a thousand times. People would start honking their horns, but I didn't know whether to turn or go straight. I'd have to pull over, and wait to regain my senses.

Then I realized that I was driving without looking in my mirrors. I was just staring straight ahead of me, as if I had tunnel vision. On a few occasions I unthinkingly passed another car unexpectedly and scared people, almost causing accidents.

One Saturday afternoon, I was driving the kids into town. We were on a highway in the old Jetta, the three of them in the back, when I happened to glance at the speedometer. I was doing 150 and pushing faster. It hit me in the gut how dangerous this was for my children. I slowed right down and I decided to get rid of my car. From then on, I would take the train back and forth from Ottawa on the weekends.

On September 18, 1998, I was scheduled to make a major presentation to the faculty and board of governors of the Royal Military College in Kingston on rethinking how we developed our officers.

I had a plan as to how the college could push for more intellectual depth in the officer corps: I was going to propose that all officers be required to earn an undergraduate degree and, as they moved up, a graduate degree. In this way, we would achieve a much better balance between intellectual and experiential knowledge. I also planned to argue that the Canadian Forces needed a separate institute that focused on research to provide guidance on developing leaders.*

---

* I was eventually successful in creating the Canadian Forces Leadership Institute. It has done incredible work bringing administration, operations and ethics closer together. With all of my failures, this is something I am quite proud of.

Less enthusiastically, I was also going to brief them on the continued major budget cuts, and how they would affect the college. I was not looking forward to the inevitable distress this would cause.

The night before, I reviewed my notes for the presentations, and filled my suitcases with paperwork. The next morning at 0500 hours I jumped in my rental car and set off on the two-and-a-half-hour drive to Kingston, grabbing a donut along the way.

I arrived and gave my first briefing to the governing body of the college at 0800. After a long question-and-answer session, I went to meet with the commandant. He had served with me, so we knew each other very well, and we had a fruitful discussion on how we saw the future development of the officer corps in these complex times. That same morning, I also forcefully presented the idea of establishing a spiritual centre for the Canadian Forces at RMC, a place where ethics and guiding moral principles could be established to assist young officers with the complex decision-making inherent in our new missions. I had even brought the chaplain-general along to press the point. But no one showed much interest in this matter. They seemed more interested in building accommodations than building a greater ethos in our future forces.

I was able to grab half a sandwich before I was whisked off to the main auditorium to speak to the faculty: the professorial corps, the research fellows, assistants, the works. Here was their opportunity to hear from the horse's mouth that the college was staying alive, but also that there were going to be more cuts. After that, I met with some post-grad students to talk about conflict for an hour or so. Then I was back in the car to Ottawa.

I got to my apartment at around 1830 hours. I'd been on the go since four in the morning and I was pretty tired. Waiting for me were big briefcases filled with new work. On days I was not in the office, my staff would bring the piled-up paperwork to my apartment so I could complete it in the night.

I'd grabbed a hot dog and had just sat down to work when the phone rang. It was Maurice. He told me he had received a call from a colleague who had been at my briefing that day. She had been worried I wasn't myself, that I had been strained and seemed down. Because he was one of the few in the senior leadership who understood the effects of PTSD, he was concerned.

"Meo, how are you feeling?" he asked.

"Well, I'm a little tired. I had the international tribunal, you know, and now the running of the shop, the reforms, the budget cuts . . ."

He interrupted to suggest, "Why don't you take a week's leave?"

"I can't do that." I actually laughed.

"In fact," he said, "I think you should take a *month*."

I was shocked into silence.

"This is suicide by work," he said firmly. "It may take a little longer, but it is just as deadly as the other means. I can't let that happen to you. When we pulled you out of Rwanda, you were a skeleton of yourself, like a bungee cord stretched to the limit. And I see it again now. I only wish I had noticed sooner. I'm sorry, *mon ami*.

"You were always so good; the best of the best, a pearl, a star. I thought work would save you. Work is what saved me when I came out of it. But you never did come out of Rwanda, did you? No, not on the inside. It is like you have been swimming in the waves: your head comes out for a bit, but then it sinks back under. Well, I will not let you drown."

"I can handle it," I insisted.

"No, I don't think you can. You need to take some time and catch your breath."

He was my friend, but he was also my superior. And this was an order.

I was hugely surprised. I honestly thought I'd been effective at hiding my condition in public, especially at work. His words hit me hard and I experienced a sudden release of all the incredible pent-up pressure I'd been suppressing while on duty. I began to cry, right there on the phone.

There was a part of me that felt a huge sense of relief that I'd been found out. Like back in Rwanda toward the end, when they'd finally recognized I was not at my best. But I was also heart-broken. I'd done it again: I felt like I'd failed. I had had to leave Rwanda because I couldn't take it, and now I was abandoning my post again.

The next morning, I went to the office and kept the door closed, because I couldn't help crying. I had initiated dozens of new pro-jects and policies, each aimed at improving quality of life for the troops and their families. Things like guaranteeing the repatria-tion of dead soldiers, the creation of a national military cemetery, ensuring medals were presented in person and no longer sent in the mail, and convincing the medical system to advertise their services, rather than waiting for the troops to seek them out. In the middle of all these important changes, I was being forced—by my own injury—to abandon it all.

It was one of the most horrible of days: September 19, 1998. My injured brain told me that I had been no good in the field and that now I was no good back home. I would have protested loudly if an injured soldier had told me he was thinking this way, but I had no defence against my own thoughts.

I wrote a letter to the 4,500 people under my command, explain-ing what had happened and why I was taking a sick leave. I gave them my address, so they could touch base if they needed to. It was very important for me to maintain that connection with them, and to know that they still had that with me. I assured them that I'd be back.

That night I stayed in my apartment, alone, as usual. I didn't pick up the phone. I didn't want to speak to anybody. I drank myself into oblivion.

CHAPTER THREE

'Twas sad as sad could be . . .

DON'T REMEMBER HOW I got to Quebec City, but I found myself in my family home. I spent my days in pyjamas. I did a lot of crying. I remember almost nothing of that time, a one-month sick leave that stretched to seven.

I know I took the train back to Ottawa for one-on-one therapy a few times, but otherwise I sat and stared, tears rolling down my face. The family was there, but I wasn't—not really. So, they attempted to go about their normal life, tiptoeing around the bath-robed lunatic weeping in the corner.

I didn't understand what was going on with me. It had been four years since the genocide. Why was this happening now?

I recalled a conversation I'd had a few months earlier, with a young major who had approached me after a talk I'd given at the Canadian Forces Staff College. "I wondered if you had a few minutes, sir," he said. "There's something I'd sure like to discuss with you, if you have the time."

He looked so distraught, I immediately guided him away from the crowds, and into an alcove in the mess.

"I'm sorry, sir. But I just don't know what's happening to me."

I recognized his face — he was a combat arms officer — but also his eyes: he was a man on the brink.

"Where did you serve, major?" I asked him.

"The Gulf, sir. 1991. I was seconded to the British forces. It's been seven years, sir, and I've been getting along just great, you know. Fine. But . . . I don't know, suddenly, it's like something is taking me over. I'm having a hard time concentrating."

His voice broke and his eyes filled up as he looked into mine.

"We were in the desert," he said. "It was nighttime. We were driving in two battle groups, but I guess we were a bit ahead of where they thought we'd be. Well, one of our aircraft came in, moving fast. I don't know, I guess they thought we were enemy forces withdrawing. Before anyone could get on the radio to them, they attacked. Dropped a five-hundred-pound bomb at the front of my group. I was about three hundred metres back. When the dust cleared, I jumped out of my vehicle and ran forward to see if anyone was still alive. Two vehicles were burning. One had been flung on its side and ripped open, with guys inside screaming. The night was so dark, and the flames made everything inside so easy to see. The guys inside, they were frying."

He broke down, weeping.

"I never told anyone about it," he struggled to say. "I never talked about it. I never wanted to. I put it in the back of my mind."

Here was a solid leader and combat solider, revealing emotions that he worried could jeopardize his career. I marvelled at his courage, his confidence in coming to me with this. I was surprised by his trust, and humbled. He had to go back to class, so he stoically composed himself, and thanked me for listening.

I told him, "You are not alone. I don't have a solution for you yet. But you are never alone."

Seven years. That's how long he held it in. That's how long the pain of this injury took to force its way out.

Now here I was, four years on, mired in my own depths. I had gone beyond drowning in anguish and anger. I had drowned. I felt like there was nothing left inside me, no heart, no guts, no soul. Just ashes and tears.

I couldn't concentrate, couldn't even pick up a newspaper. I couldn't muster the willpower to get out the door, even just to run to the store. I couldn't summon the effort required to dress.

People often think that the one thing that will help you is to get out and have a good time. This couldn't be further from the truth. I couldn't laugh, I couldn't feel happy even for a minute. I looked around me, and everything was affected by what I had seen in Rwanda. My values had changed and my criteria for what was positive or good in the world had changed, too. I just didn't want to engage in a way of life that didn't make any sense to me, with its hypocrisy, its unnecessary self-indulgence. Also even if I had wanted to "put the past aside for a few hours," as people begged me to do, there was no way I could, because someone inevitably would raise it. I couldn't blend in. So there was no way of . . . being normal. The medication and the therapy had not rendered me capable of rejoining this world.

In this devastated condition, I found it strange to have my wife and kids around me. I had tried to protect them from my suffering. For four years I'd worked myself into the ground, as horrible images, sounds and smells invaded my mind twenty-four hours a day. Throughout those years I had driven a thousand kilometres every weekend I could to be with them, and now here I was day in, day out, crashed, broken, useless. I had to wonder what life would have been like if my wife had brought the kids to Ottawa and we'd established a home together. Would I have been able to handle this injury better by now? God knows.*

I suppose I could have insisted at some point, but I thought Beth's arguments made sense for the wellbeing of the kids—keep them out of the spotlight, and in their established routine. The price for their stability during these years was, clearly, my isolation. Beth would argue that I was the one who found ways to stay away from home, and that even when I was with them, I was distant. She told me I'd been gone ever since I left for Africa. And she was right. I had put them through so much already.

Musing on it now, though, I think I hadn't insisted they join me because I had been afraid to have that fight. What if I had asked and they had refused? I was so screwed up, and I didn't want to subject them to more of it. And yet, now, here we all were—trapped together in the house, and me more of a burden than ever.

My wife had found me difficult, and moody, even before this breakdown. Now, whenever she could rouse me out of my stupor

***

* Twenty years later, I received an email from my youngest child, who is the only member of my family who has read Shake Hands with the Devil: The Failure of Humanity in Rwanda (the book in which I detailed my mission). He had been undergoing anger management therapy, not only because of what the mission did to me, but what my PTSD did to our family. In that email he asked me, "Why did we stay in Quebec City when we were kids? Why didn't we move to be with you? Wouldn't it have been better for all of us? For us, but also for you?" I didn't know how to respond.

to talk about even the most minor of household issues, our discussions would often get heated. The minute I expressed any kind of emotion, she would interrupt me to ask if I'd taken my pills. This was her way of telling me that I was being irrational, and needed to medicate so I could communicate more reasonably. She was understandably frustrated with me, but I felt this as dismissive and hurtful.

I received little support from my colleagues and peers; I received only a few messages from my sixty or so fellow generals—a couple of phone calls, and an email from one old friend. The others appeared to be in two camps: those who were too busy to get in touch, and those who didn't know what to say.

I had one visitor: Maurice. He came and sat by me in the living room, him in his uniform, me in my dressing gown. We sat and I cried and cried and cried.

It was Maurice who brought me back from that limbo. After six months, I was more functional—I suppose from the therapy, and the medication was doing its thing. But the question remained, functional for what? What do you do with a three-star general who is injured and, according to the medical staff, psychologically very limited in what he can handle?

Luckily, Maurice was in my corner. He approached a junior colleague of ours and told him, "I want you to create terms of reference for Roméo. Something not too stressful, but long-term, where he will only have to work half days. We can ease his return, and from there we'll see what happens."

By April 1999, I was back in Ottawa as special adviser to the chief of defence staff. When Maurice handed me my terms of reference, he told me, "Take your time with it. You are on half days, as the doctor suggested. Think about this, and we will decide how far we want to go with it."

It was a one-page instruction to examine the officer corps, to get at the deficiencies that we had picked up on in Somalia and the changes that we had initiated, which had not yet made their way throughout the psyche of the corps. Basically, I was to consider what *is* the officer corps of the future and what are the skill sets and knowledge and experience officers need to handle that future. Maurice felt it was something that I would be good at. He knew I was interested in leadership development and ethics, and he knew quite a bit about the direction I was thinking because I had been so vocal—both to members of the Forces and at staff colleges, as well as pro bono in speeches on civvy street. It nagged at me that I was not able to go back to my old job, but I was glad to have the uniform back on. I felt safe being back in the military milieu, and glad to have an interesting challenge that I believed in.

They had intended merely to accommodate me and my injury, inventing something easy for me to do. But by week's end, I had created a work plan and a proposal to reform the officer corps and the entire leadership development structure.

Maurice was not surprised at my zeal—he always said I was the visionary and he was the tactical guy. He gave me the staff I requested: a secretary, an executive assistant, and an assortment of majors and lieutenant-colonels, almost all with PhDs. This was an unusual, outspoken and opinionated bunch, well-versed in the Forces and hungry for a real challenge. The team fully grasped the deficiencies and the obstacles we were facing, and their inventiveness in tackling the problems knew no bounds. Together, we decided to blow the whole thing wide open. This was incredibly rewarding work, and I don't think I lasted more than a few days as part-time. I was in it full blast.

—

Within two weeks, I was back to working twenty hours a day and passing out at my desk. I was back to speaking nightly, back to attending conferences, back to the international legal fights. Of course, our work—we called it "Officer 2020"—was urgent and essential, but I know now that the fervour with which I approached it came from a deeper, and wounded, place.

I had come back from the pit of hell, where I had suffered this injury, and had continued to fight on nearly all fronts: my colleagues and the military system, the harsh criticism of my command decisions in Rwanda, the testimony in Luc's court martial and the tribunal. Other guys go through this, and they turn to booze or drugs. Some isolate themselves and become hermits. Still others kill themselves. I worked.

I worked and worked, and the more I worked, the more work multiplied. And the more it multiplied, the less I could handle it. On top of the speeches and conferences on Rwanda, the volume and scale of work at the office was off the map. There was no way to sustain it. I was keeping two campaigns going: one for the troops and their well-being, and one for the Rwandan people.

I wondered why I never said, "Enough! No more!" Why did I keep agreeing to talk, why did I keep pushing, forcing people to remember the genocide, fighting for the troops, fighting for quality of life, for a better medical system, when it was not serving me? Why didn't I just stay home and go sell shoes at the local shopping centre?

The therapists kept telling me that if anyone had the right to say *enough*, it was me. But then what? What would I do if I stopped working? What would I do to withstand the guilt? I just could not (and will never) get to the point of saying, "I've done

my bit and now it's time for something else." Command responsibility never left me. My concern with the 24/7 continuum of
operations in Rwanda remained, as the guys who had served
under me in Rwanda were still serving. They were still influenc-
ing my work, driving me to continue to look out for them now, as
I had in the field.

My therapists and I questioned whether, as Maurice had said,
I had an unconscious desire to work myself to death, pushing
my body in order to crash it again. To self-destruct. I began to
comprehend this aspect of my injury, but even so, I continued
pushing, pushing, pushing. Not only did I dive into Officer 2020
with manic fanaticism, I also pulled out a lot of my initiatives
that had been either partly implemented or shoved entirely to the
wayside in the seven months I'd been away.

I believed, rightly, that so much needed to be done. But I
believed, *wrongly*, that I was doing my job, and doing it better
and better. To others, it looked like I was shooting in all directions: no one could follow me.

In the third week of December 1999, after I had been back on the
job eight months, Maurice called me to his office.

"How is it going?" he asked me.

I started to brief him on the Officer 2020 draft, but he interrupted me. "We are quite worried about you, you know. You are
driving yourself into the ground again. This was supposed to be
part-time."

He said that my reform project was very interesting, even
essential, but it was far more than I should be doing. "I'd thought
that if we brought you back, that this time we could protect you,
instead of exploiting you. I thought we could benefit from your
talent and your vision and help you at the same time. But you are

also still working hard on Rwanda. I'm afraid you can't do both. I'm afraid it is killing you."

I met his eye. "I've said it before—if it's a choice of keeping my career or keeping the Rwandan genocide alive, there is no question."

"We are quite conscious that you cannot sustain this," he countered. "You need one hundred percent of your time to heal yourself, and get professional help. The surgeon-general has come to me with a written report that your injury is not getting better. I'm sorry," he said, "but I can't keep a three-star who can't be deployed."

He handed me a piece of paper on which it was written that I was no longer fit to command troops in operations. That phrase was devastating. He showed me the accompanying medical report, a thick stack of forms that all boiled down to one sentence: "Member's medical condition precludes employment in a military operational environment."[*]

Thirty-six years of commanding and leading troops; of preparing for and participating in operations; of truth, duty and valour: a piece of paper ended it with a single line.

This piece of paper was a stark contrast to the evaluation report I'd received in July 1994, toward the end of my mission in Rwanda. It had been labelled "OUTSTANDING":

MGen Dallaire's physical stamina and endurance since the tragedy began in Rwanda on 6 April have been an example

---

[*] Although most three-star generals only do staff work, the Canadian Forces has a requirement called universality of service: every commander must be capable of being deployed in the field. Because they'd decided I was not fit to command troops in theatre, they had to get rid of me entirely. *"Étant donné que le maintien en fonction ou le reclassement ne peuvent être considerés, la libération est la seule alternative."*

> *to the world and a great credit to Canada and the Canadian*
> *Forces. . . . responded magnificently . . . courageous . . . excep-*
> *tional . . . idolized by his troops from all nations. . . . MGen*
> *Dallaire remains a positive, cheerful, tower of strength, always*
> *exuding confidence and enthusiasm. . . . clearly demonstrated*
> *considerable potential for continued advancement . . .*

When that report had been written, I had already been injured. Since then, I'd somehow gone from these accolades to an assessment that deemed me incapacitated, no matter how keen I was to work. If ever there was an example of how this injury grows over time, it was this.

I knew it made all kinds of sense, but it really, really hurt. I had been in the army since the day I was born, my father arriving in a jeep and uniform to see me and his Dutch war bride at the hospital in Holland at the end of the Second World War. In my youth in Canada, we'd lived in wartime housing. Many of my teachers, brothers of the Order of St. Gabriel, were reserve officers, and my school had a rifle range in the basement. By fifteen, I was leading army cadets, and for the next three decades, I commanded troops. It was the essence of my life.

Because of my upbringing—no love to speak of, a father who did not spare the rod, a stress on duty and chores—I've found it foreign to express affection for people in my personal life, even when I felt it. But it was not foreign for me to love the army or the soldiers under my command. And now I had been told I couldn't be trusted to lead them any longer. To a commander, this is inconceivable.

That was actually the moment that I realized, *viscerally*, that I had been injured. Seven months of crying on the couch on sick leave hadn't really done it, but that one phrase brought it all home. I was never going to command troops again. My injury had destroyed my career and my raison d'être.

I could hear Maurice talking, as if from far away.

"I don't want you to leave immediately; we want to find someone good to replace you because this is good work.* Roméo, take three months to prepare for your departure."

I spent my last day at National Defence headquarters, clearing out my desk, trying to draw out the time I spent packing, signing last-minute documents, and saying goodbye to my staff. It was April 18, 2000. I chose that date for my medical release from the army because it was one of the few days in April with a positive association—my wife's birthday.

---

* Under my successor, my team kept working on Officer 2020 for another year or so, but the team was ultimately disbanded. By the time they saw the next draft, it was so watered down they couldn't recognize it. A few years later, though, I got a call from the minister of national defence, John McCallum. He was a solid guy, and very interested in pedagogy. He arrived at the restaurant where he'd asked to meet incognito, with no staff car and no aide-de-camp. He sat down and reached into his jacket pocket, pulling out my original executive summary. "Do you remember this?" he asked. "Yes, that's my draft, from back in January 2000," I replied. "Well, I've got something on my desk today that doesn't make any sense. It's crap. It doesn't have a clear objective; it doesn't have a clear plan. However, this," he said, "has it all. I want to implement *this* draft." So we talked long and hard about it. I gave him a lot of background material, and he went off to make the reforms I had originally suggested. Finally, after all these years, a success! Unfortunately, soon after that meeting there was a cabinet shuffle, and he was no longer minister of defence. The staff was then able to minimize the reform so that it wouldn't cost much or disrupt much. The antithesis of the exercise.

Since I'd returned from Rwanda, April was always a hard month because it marked the anniversary of the start of the genocide. I was especially sensitive and emotionally vulnerable. I was terrified of being at home with nothing to take my mind off the memories, but my doctors were recommending no work, no testimonies, no speeches.

If I thought those first six years had been hard, I had another think coming.

When the uniform came off, the separation felt violent; the system, to which I had spent a lifetime being loyal, was breaking its loyalty to me. Every reference point was gone. There was nothing positive in my life. My mind reeled with panic and fear as I contemplated a life out of the army.

I recalled the late 1960s, when the government had made major cuts to the military and started giving out golden handshakes under the name Operation Restore. After a few years, we serving members started to get notes from our regiments that so-and-so had died. And then another so-and-so had died. Holy smokes, I remember realizing, these guys were only in their fifties. We soon worked out that their "retirement" from everything that gave them their sense of fraternity, of understanding, of purpose, of security, had totally destroyed them. They were dying of a broken heart.

In the days and nights that followed my departure from the military, the madness of the past five years jumbled in my brain. I came out of Rwanda broken, having been relieved of command because I had nothing left to give, but within two weeks I was thrust into a series of high-requirement jobs at a time of enormous crisis in the Canadian military. I was carrying this Rwandan legacy that nobody in power wanted to know about, but that I kept insisting on telling anyone who would listen. I received nothing positive out of it—not money (all my speeches were pro bono), not comfort (it was like picking at a scab), not satisfaction (nothing substantive had changed for Rwanda or the world after years and years of testifying and speech-making). In all that time, I said yes to every request, every interview, every additional responsibility, no matter how potentially damning or damaging to me personally.

By this point, my experience in Rwanda had been pathologized: it's the best way I can think to describe it. During the height of the genocide, there was no time off, there was no stopping, there was no sleep. Everything was so terribly urgent, I couldn't *not* work. All day, all night, all the time. Since I came home I had been behaving in exactly the same way: I did every single thing that anyone ever asked me to do. And now the army had stopped asking.

I had absolutely no idea what life was like out of uniform. I had no interest in puttering around the house and working in the garden; my father, a relentless and tyrannical chore-setter, had made me hate those things. Golfing and fishing? No. Going to the garrison club, drinking gin and playing dominoes all day? No. With nothing to do, I had nothing to keep my memories at bay. And soon I was adrift in a sea of torment and loss. I didn't even know how to dress. I didn't know what to do with my uniforms. They, and the traditions they represented, had been my safety net. The uniforms had come off, but I was still khaki inside. I desperately needed a mission.

Since I couldn't break the lease, I kept the Ottawa apartment. I spent the next months there, in a drunken blur, grabbing at any little scrap of work I could find. It wasn't for the money; for me, that has never been a reason. I despise money—you can't imagine how much. But I had nothing left. No soul, no reason for living.

I was aching, terrified, tormented, desperate, so I began filling my schedule with more and more speaking engagements, anywhere that would have me: everything from the Pearson Peacekeeping Centre in Cornwallis to the ladies' auxiliary in Guelph. I set up meetings with Veterans Affairs on veterans' mental health, with the minister of defence on the Unknown Soldier project. I jumped on boards of organizations, the garrison club, the regimental senate.

Over those first weeks, within this bedlam of activity, it occurred to me that I could now, must now, devote every ounce of energy I had to Rwanda. I would write a book. A book that detailed every moment I could recall. I could set the record straight and perhaps bring closure to my troubled soul. Or would the effort rip me open once and for all? I met with agents and publishers and journalists to embark on this project, which sometimes struck me as a descent into hell, and sometimes as a resurrection from it.

So, my days were soon chock-a-block—therefore, successfully distracting. But my nights, those dreadful nights, those heavy, pulsing, crushing nights, turned my busy desperation into pure madness.

It felt like an unseen hand had captured me and was holding me firmly in a grip from which I could not escape. Each night I was absorbed by the black ink of darkness, abandoned, but for the hundreds of thousands of murdered souls who haunted me, subsumed me. In that darkness, I was primed to relive every possible moment that came to mind or to invade my soul, preventing me from even imagining that I could live without the constant reminder of those atrocities and of my inability to stop the genocide.

One evening, after a late therapy session (in which once again I was told, "You did everything you could") and a presentation (in front of a crowd of two hundred people yet feeling so alone), I went back to my apartment and slumped in a chair with a bottle of Scotch. With heavy hands, I hauled my plastic pill organizer out of my briefcase. Turning it over, toying with it, while I drank straight from the bottle, I was bursting with the sounds and sights I had just—with such succinct efficiency—retold. If they only knew. Those people sat and listened, then stood and applauded, but they didn't know the half of it. About Rwanda, or about me. I popped open one of the little compartments, and overturned the container. A little rainbow of five pills tumbled into my hand. I opened the next compartment, and the next. Fifteen little pills. Tossing these into my mouth, I chased them with the Scotch, then emptied the rest of the box into my mouth. Then I stumbled to the bathroom and pulled out the five orange plastic prescription bottles, and one of Aspirin, and some old Tylenol 3s I had left over from when my arm had acted up.

Tears came again as I contemplated the agony of all those deaths, all that horror. In the mirror, I mocked my therapists' attempts at comfort: what is saving thousands as we had done, when nearly a million died and hundreds of thousands of others perished in the aftermath?

I retched, as I thought about accepting the applause that night, after I had challenged those unsuspecting people to think about what it truly means to say that every human is human and no one is more human than another. Yet I had played God over life and death, while so many were crushed like insects.

I had done a hellish thing,
And it would work 'em woe.

I swallowed the pills, I drank the Scotch, I lay down, weeping, waiting for the end.

The next morning, I awoke in a pile of sick. I couldn't even kill myself.

In the weeks that followed that suicide attempt I travelled even more. I would give my talk in front of ever-growing crowds, and then go straight to my hotel room and lock myself in with a bottle. Often, I would drink until I passed out, but other times rage would overtake me, and I would rip the phone out of the socket, smash the lamps, tear up the towels, screaming all the while.

Something would eventually stop me. A noise from the hall or the morning light through the window would pull me out of the spiral. Then I'd just slump down among the mess, with tear-filled eyes.

Those bust-ups didn't feel good. They just left me feeling even sadder.

One night, in my own apartment and drunk and full of rage again, I smashed all my Rwanda stuff. I smashed the statues, tore the paintings. I swept my arms across the coffee table, sending glass and papers flying. Stumbling thickly, stupidly, over to the sliding glass doors that led to my eighth-floor balcony, I was going to throw myself off.

An old wooden rocking chair blocked my way; I kicked at it, and when it bounced back at me I roared with mindless fury and knocked it over on its side. Then I tried to kick the back off it, but my foot caught between the slats. I tried to get out on the balcony, but couldn't shake off what remained of the chair, and it wouldn't fit through the sliding door.

As I was struggling, I heard the key turn in the front door. It was my niece, who ran to me. She untangled me, and put me to bed.

When my sister-in-law heard about this, she put me on extreme watch. They hadn't been coming over so much since I'd got back from my exile in Quebec City. Now, one of them came almost every day. I didn't burden the girls with my rantings, but Christine again became a valued sounding board, especially after my weekly therapy session. Of course, she had her own life, all three of them did, and they could not—nor should they have been—with me at all times.

One evening when I had had no speech to give, I took a long shower, and then sat in my easy chair, sipping Scotch, alone. I knew another bout of binge drinking wouldn't soothe the overwhelming sadness I was feeling and I turned on the stereo.

I listened to the Gordon Lightfoot song about the old soldier who dies in the street. It seemed to me not such a horrible fate. My therapists had suggested that my wish to end my life was an attempt to cop out on my responsibilities and the expectations placed on me. But I didn't agree. I knew the suicide attempts were about escaping from the pain. That is all I wanted: relief from the pain. I wanted that pain to stop.

We use that term "gut-wrenching" to describe grief or anguish, but it's not your stomach that's hurting (if it were only that, Gaviscon could help). It is deeper, in your soul, but it is real, physical pain. I remember, a lifetime ago, laughing so hard I felt it in my gut. I had not felt that way since Rwanda. Now there was pain instead. People who mourn one death can feel incredible pain. Multiply the feeling by eight hundred thousand, and imagine the weight of that.

I sat in that chair, thinking about Rwanda. Thinking about the army. Thinking about all the soldiers before me. My father-in-law. My dad.

I recalled the old metal box of my dad's, in which I had stored the ribbons of his medals and some other stuff of his. I went into my room to retrieve it. Opening it up for the first time in over a decade, I found his old doubled-edged shaving razor inside. There was still a blade in it.

I went back and sat on the sofa, then slid down onto the floor with my feet under the coffee table, and leaned back against the sofa. Very deliberately, very slowly, I started to cut into the tops of my thighs. With every cut, a warmth; a soothing, intoxicating smell. With every cut, I defeated the horror. With every cut, I released the devil, the demons, the angry souls, the oh-so-real pain of sadness, guilt, failure, accusations, defeat.

Blood oozed out of me in long trickles of red warmth. It was the closest I had come in years to a feeling of bliss and freedom. I cut and cut, my thighs then my arms, ever so slowly. There was not a lot of blood, just those easing trickles of blissful release. I was being set free in some sort of way.

A knock on the door. My sister-in-law.

After that night, I decided to give up on suicide. It was clearly not going to work for me.

> 'The man hath penance done,
> And penance more will do.'

My demise—that final sleep that would finally end this life that never should have survived the mission—would have to come some other way than by my hand, as clearly I was no good at it. But anything I could do to precipitate it, I must. I had spent years trying to work myself to death, and now work had been taken from me. Would I end up in an alley with a bottle in my hand? Would I finally find a way to push myself beyond where I had already gone? Or was there a way to incite death at someone else's hand?

Rwanda, July 1994

Peace is breaking out all over, but the ugliness of what has happened remains. Evidence, in the shape of corpses, tells of their last moments. Elderly people, a pregnant woman — mid-breech, split open and broken in the mud and the rain. Tens of thousands of people hacked down while running for their lives, or trampled to death by the terror-stricken. You can see from their expressions, even in death, that they were not resigned. That they died asking, "How is this possible? I had nothing to do with this. I don't understand."

I've been on the phone to New York for weeks, trying to convince the DPKO to find a replacement for me as force commander. It's a little early for a change in command, but I've brought us through the worst of it. I can step aside without putting the mission at risk; I cannot stay and say the same. All the signs are there: the irritability, the lack of control over emotions, the lack of objectivity — they all point to a soldier at the end of his tether. I've seen it in my troops but now that soldier is me.

The things we've all witnessed are horrific, yes, but the things really wearing me down are particular to being in command: the frustrations, the lies, the abandonment, the mission gone awry, the failure to protect, the inability to influence. All this is creeping on me. So I write and I call and I try to convince them I am a liability—that they have to replace me. And yet they ask me to stay on. At first, because they need me; now, because the person they have in mind to replace me is still walking the corridors at UN headquarters.

The fighting continues, though the worst of it is over. It has to be—practically everyone is dead. Bodies are everywhere, like dogshit in Paris, like litter in Delhi, like the stench of filthy oil in East End Montreal; there isn't a square metre void of bones shrouded in varying degrees of decaying flesh. There are still extremists around. Now that there are no more Tutsi or moderate Hutus for them to kill, they have orders to kill me, and any of the other few remaining obstacles. We hear it screamed over the radio: *"Tuez Dallaire!"*

I stand on the rooftop of the compound, aware of the way the lights silhouette me. I light my cigar, holding the flame longer than necessary, giving them time to aim. "Do your worst," I think.

Several times, I shake my escort and head for the vehicles in the compound. I quickly jump in one of

them and take off. I drive through the darkness, down
back roads, through villages, bush areas, plantations.
I don't clear my route with anyone. I browbeat my way
through checkpoints. Fucked-up kids, high as kites,
armed to the teeth, shove rifles in my face, screaming at
me in Kinyarwanda. I stare them down and drive
through, daring them, willing them, to fire. Sometimes
they do, the bullets pinging off the metal body of my
vehicle, but nothing ever hits me.

Having come through so much killing and destruction without a scratch, I am filled with defiance. It is
impossible that I will leave Rwanda without being
injured. I feel I have to bear something more than
fatigue and stress. I cannot leave here alive.

After having survived a number of ambushes at the
height of the war, I am now actively seeking them out.
I have entirely lost that healthy fear you need to stay
alive. "They won't hit me," I think to myself. "They
can't hit me. The bullet hasn't been made that can kill
me!" I am taunting death as I actively seek it out.

I've seen such cockiness get people killed, and here I
am, the force commander, acting this way. It is totally
unheard-of behaviour; it is dangerous and it is deterio-
rating. My initial request for release, based on my ability
to sustain the work, has turned very rapidly into me
losing it.

On one particular occasion, I am approaching a
checkpoint with a crude barrier arm—a thin tree trunk
propped across the road. A teenage girl stands in front of
it, a machine gun cocked and raised in her thin arms.
I am driving fast, and I am armed. She sees me coming,
and she knows. She knows I'm not going to stop.

I couldn't sleep—didn't want to sleep. So, around midnight or
one o'clock in the morning, I pulled on my grubbiest old clothes
and I went out walking in the big park by the river right outside
my apartment building. It was quiet; none of the usual joggers or
sightseers were in the park at night. I restlessly wandered in the
darkness, hoping to be mugged.

I'd walked that park for years, following the main path, and sat
for hours on the benches by the river. Now I wandered further,
explored deeper, coming to the parts of the trail where it met a
series of subtle footpaths people had made through the bushes
and trees, into the woods and down to the water's edge. I pressed
my way along, gently pushing aside branches, hoping to be
ambushed. Hoping there'd be some deranged person who would
knife me, or some guys looking for money who would beat me up.

Night after night, I returned, seeking ambush, dishonour or
death in these woods. I walked in the rain, in the snow. Freezing.
Waiting for death. I could be out there roaming about for four or
five hours in the night. And then, inevitably, beautifully, thankfully, there would come the sound of a bird, or a sliver of silver
dawn in the night's darkness: that first light that only the roosters
usually see. It always came, and with it a promise, the faintest hint
of optimism. I would fall out of my self-destructive daze. I could
rejoin the living, for another day.

CHAPTER FOUR

I closed my lids, and kept them close
And the balls like pulses beat;
For the sky and the sea, and the sea and the sky
Lay like a load on my weary eye
And the dead were at my feet.

L YING ON MY STOMACH in the wet grass next to the park bench, I feel the mud bleeding through the knees of my trousers and the front of my shirt. Everything is spinning, but I can just make out the blurry yellow lights of my apartment building on the other side of the park. They seem so distant, unreachable.

Defeated, I cry out, "Kill me! Please, kill me!"

I hear footsteps, voices, and then an ambulance siren echoing through the darkness.

As usual, I hadn't slept much the night before—perhaps three tormented hours. I had spent the day making calls, giving a newspaper interview over the phone, preparing for a presentation and taking care of some urgent paperwork, then attending an afternoon event at the Department of Foreign Affairs on genocide prevention. There, I'd shaken hands with MPs, chatted with some old colleagues, paid the proper degree of attention to the assorted VIPs. I'd gone home afterward, and worked until it was time for my weekly therapy appointment at 1800 hours.

These sessions were always hard, but some were harder than others. My therapist and I hadn't even begun to discuss how to cope with what I was now living through. Now, out of uniform after thirty-six years, I felt completely abandoned, as if my unit were marching ahead to continue its assault on the enemy but I couldn't go with it: I'd been injured and left behind. I was trying to grasp reality and how to face the day, every day, and at the same time as I was dealing with the fact that I had become a liability to the institution that had been my calling. In therapy, we were still tearing brutal, ugly, painful memories of the genocide from my entrails, on the theory that once that was done, some day in the future, my doctor could begin to create a therapeutic plan for me.

As usual, I'd left her office red-eyed and shaking. Instead of grabbing a cab home, I found myself walking aimlessly through the streets. About to pass a liquor store, I stopped instead and went inside. I stood before the shelves of Scotch for a long time, and then stepped away. But I needed something to numb my mind. Quickly I turned back and grabbed a forty-ouncer.

On the street, I felt exposed, embarrassed to be carrying that tell-tale brown bag. The sidewalk to my right led to the river, the bridge, and my apartment. To my left was the path to the National War Memorial. I turned left and walked slowly, as if compelled, to the granite arch and bronze sculptures of *The Response*.

I had been closely involved in the repatriation of the Canadian Tomb of the Unknown Soldier from Vimy Ridge in France to the base of the War Memorial in Ottawa. Just a few weeks earlier the tomb had finally come home, but I had yet to visit it. Now I sat on a stone bench beside this extraordinary monument, not drinking, just looking up at the winged glory of Peace, at the heavy strength of the soldiers marching through the arch in their great response to the call to war. Here, communing with them and with the soul of the unknown Canadian who died in battle overseas so long ago, I felt safe. For over an hour, I sat there, tears streaming down my face, reflecting on the many "unknowns" I could put names to, the men and women and children who had been slaughtered. I also relived the losses of the troops under my command, feeling the unending burden of that responsibility.

Eventually, I stood up and walked toward the bridge.

Christine had been at my apartment waiting for me to come back from therapy. When I didn't arrive she jumped in her car to look for me. She was driving toward me now, about to cross the bridge into Ottawa as I was walking across it in the opposite direction. She pulled over and called to me from the window, "*Embarque!*" *Get in!* She threw open the passenger side door.

I slammed it shut and waved her off. She was forced by the traffic to drive on, but she called that she would circle back and meet me at the apartment.

But I didn't head home. Instead, I followed the pedestrian path into the park by the woods.

It was a warm summer evening, and the sun was setting. I sat on a bench with the woods and the river's edge behind me. The encroaching night was quiet enough that I could hear the sound of water lapping through the trees.

With determination, I opened the bottle. I finished it in less than an hour. My aim was to get good and plastered—to erase everything in my mind with the booze, to become blank, numb.

I sat on that park bench for hours after the bottle was empty, scenes of the genocide creeping in through the blur of alcohol and pills. When I finally staggered upright, my head was swimming, my stomach in knots, my soul withered. It was so dark I couldn't make out anything but the lights of my apartment building across the park. I took a few unsteady steps toward those lights, able to hold on to only one thought. To end this. To end me.

As I shuffled from the asphalt path to the grass, I stumbled and fell. Unable to get up, I crawled forward with a singular aim: to reach my building and find a way to end my suffering. But in my mindless drunken state, the building seemed to be getting farther and farther away as I inched toward it. I collapsed in despair, my addled mind convinced that reaching it was impossible.

"Please, please!" Sobs distorted my voice, as I struggled through that endless expanse of grass. "Kill me! Anybody, please, get it over with! Kill me."

"Kill me," I begged the EMT who gently turned me over, and lifted me onto a gurney.

"Kill me!" I pleaded with Christine, who was at my side when I came out of sedation in hospital the next day.

On June 28, 2000, the CBC reported that I'd been found, passed out, in the park:

> Retired Lieutenant-General Roméo Dallaire was found
> semi-conscious on a park bench in Hull on Tuesday. The
> Quebec City native, who headed the United Nations
> mission to Rwanda in 1994, was taken to hospital appar-
> ently in a heavily intoxicated state.

Media across the country picked up the story, and I felt I owed the public some sort of explanation. I wrote an open letter, which was aired on July 1 on CBC Radio.

> Thank you for the very kind thoughts and wishes. There are times when the best medication and therapist simply can't help a soldier suffering from this new generation of peacekeeping injury.
>
> The anger, the rage, the hurt and the cold loneliness that separate you from your family, friends and society's normal daily routine are so powerful that the option of destroying yourself is both real and attractive. That is what happened last Monday night. It appears, it grows, it invades and it overpowers you. In my current state of therapy, which continues to show very positive results, control mechanisms have not yet matured to always be on top of this battle. My doctors and I are still building my prosthesis that will establish the level of serenity and productivity I yearn so much for.
>
> The therapists agree the battle I waged that night was a solid example of the human trying to come out from behind the military leader's ethos of "my mission first, my personnel, then myself." Obviously the venue I used last Monday night leaves a lot to be desired and will be the subject of a lot of work over the next while. I must say the

incident in question took place, for the first time, outside of my dwelling.

I do not wish to be seen as pretentious enough to speak to your listeners on the day of our national holiday; however, every one of those in military uniform who has served outside our magnificent country, comes home with a stronger desire to defend it, to love it, to protect it and to live within it with dignity and respect. Many are casualties of this last decade of world disorder. There will be new casualties amongst our ranks during the next decade and beyond.

I believe the cause for enforcing respect for individual human rights and the campaign for the establishment of human security for all are worthy missions for this country on the world stage. This nation, without any hesitation or doubt, is capable and even expected by the less fortunate of this globe to lead the developed countries beyond self-interest, strategic advantages and isolationism, and raise their sights to the realm of the pre-eminence of humanism and freedom.

The youth of our nation, volunteering to serve as soldiers, sailors and airpersons today and into the future are capable of facing up to, with their families in support, the sacrifices, the injuries and the complex moral and ethical dilemmas of peacekeeping or conflict resolution around the world. They must, however, believe their families and themselves are being treated fairly and with dignity by a nation well aware of what is at stake for them.

I believe we are on the verge of a new social contract between the members of the Canadian Armed Forces and our citizenry. A new contract for a whole new generation of dangerous and at times devastating operational missions where Canada is not at risk, but where humanitarianism is being destroyed and the innocent are being literally trampled into the ground.

The soldiers, sailors and airpersons, committing themselves and their families to carry our values, our respect for the dignity of men and women independent of any differences, supported by fellow countrymen who recognize the cost in human sacrifice and in resources, will forge in concert with our politicians, our diplomats, our resource managers and our fast-growing humanitarian agencies, a most unique and exemplary place for Canada in the league of nations, united under the United Nations Charter.

I hope this is OK. Thanks for the opportunity.

Warmest regards,
Dallaire*

---

* "Roméo Dallaire Writes," July 4, 2000. *The National Post*

I had been caught out and now, I thought, I would be deservedly disgraced. But the response to my park-bench incident—this very public humiliation followed by my hastily written apology—was the opposite of what I'd expected. Rather than being met with ridicule and scorn, I found sympathy and kindness. It seemed that by being discovered in a park, half-comatose from drink, I had instantly accomplished what I had been trying to do for years in all my profile-raising work on PTSD: normalizing this pervasive veterans' injury and granting its sufferers some measure of the respect they deserved. An unintended success.

Some media outlets did publish condemnations of me, but the tide seemed to be turning. And, because of my very public demonstration of the consequences of PTSD, more veterans reached out to me. Committees studying the injury asked for my help, too, and judges and lawyers appealed to me to help them understand and untangle cases before the courts—cases in which vets who had served in complex missions had come home changed, and now were on trial for erratic behaviour that had had criminal consequences.

At around the same time, reports on the Rwandan genocide from the Organization of African Unity, Human Rights Watch and the UN's Independent Inquiry all revealed positive aspects of my command during the genocide.*

---

*   *The Charlottetown Guardian,* July 13, 2000
    An independent panel commissioned by the Organization of African Unity charged this weekend that the United States, France and Belgium, as well as the Roman Catholic and Anglican churches, actively prevented peacekeepers from moving in to stop the mass killing of as many as 800,000 Rwandans in 1994.

    National Post, July 7, 2000
    Lt.-Gen. Dallaire's breakdown comes as his military reputation is being restored. Last December, an inquiry panel confirmed the retired general

These expert evaluations, along with a book published later that year in Canada called *The Lion, The Fox and the Eagle*, in which journalist Carol Off put together the first lengthy narrative of my mission in Rwanda, seemed to help turn public opinion of me (and of PTSD) overwhelmingly positive within the space of a few months.

When it came to the Rwandan mission, public criticism was now focused on the United Nations, rather than me personally. People were suddenly—after six years—very interested in understanding exactly what had gone wrong, and what the international community had to learn from this terrible experience. They were also very interested in learning more about how experiences like Rwanda (and Yugoslavia, and Cambodia, and Haiti . . .) were affecting our troops. I had already been doing a lot, but now I was bombarded with requests for interviews and invitations to speak not only on Rwanda, but the UN, the living conditions of military personnel, and of course PTSD.

As always, I said yes to everything asked of me. But for the first time since I'd returned from Rwanda, it seemed as though my speaking out might actually have some effect. I found that people—the public, rather than the military establishment I'd been trying to change from the inside—understood the grave urgency of these issues far better than anyone in the system had done. Inside the military, I had just been another staff officer raising shit; now that I was out of uniform, the issues that had

---

sent a telex warning the UN Security Council of a potential massacre. The inquiry blamed the United Nations, and secretary-general Kofi Annan in particular, for failing to respond to Lt.-Gen. Dallaire's request to step in to prevent the genocide. "[The UN] should also be flexible enough to allow the Force Commander the leeway to adapt to changing circumstances on the ground," the inquiry advised. A court has also exonerated Lt.-Gen. Dallaire in the deaths of the 10 Belgians. Even so, he remains frustrated by his mission's failure.

been plaguing me for so long—the failure of humanity in Rwanda, and the moral injuries that were affecting veterans of such complex missions—were starting to receive some of the attention they deserved.

Here was a real chance to make progress, and now that I was released from the military I desperately needed a mission. But once again, I took on too much. The injury plaguing my mind made it impossible for me to settle on just one of the innumerable issues I was being asked to address. Over the next two years, I agreed to join the post-Somalia ministerial education advisory board, and the Vimy Ridge rejuvenation project; I continued to participate in genocide prevention and numerous quality-of-life projects as well as a committee on the Veterans' Charter; I spent hours and hours meeting with veterans in person and listening to them on the phone. I gave active support to the nascent Canadian Armed Forces peer-support system (which was, according to anecdotal evidence, preventing a suicide a day), and I became an unofficial advocate for getting veterans in need into the system. Once they were on my radar, I was not going to let these guys slip away, but their cases required so much follow-up that I once again hired an old regimental comrade-in-arms, David Hyman, to help with the increased workload.

I also took on nuclear disarmament, child labour, aboriginal rights and small arms proliferation. I accepted the role of special adviser to the chief of defence staff. And in September 2000, I flew to Winnipeg to participate in the International Conference on War-Affected Children, hosted by the federal government and UNICEF. I gave my speech at the panel to which I'd been invited, disagreed with the other two panellists, and got quite the debate happening. The media loved it. Afterward, Maria Minna, the minister for international cooperation, who was also there, called me to her suite, where we discussed the issues of child soldiers and child protection. She liked some of my ideas, and asked for my help on the resolutions being presented. Then, to my surprise, she offered me a job as her child-protection adviser. Of course, I didn't know how much this work would come to mean to me in the future. I *did* know that the part-time salary would mean I could stay on at my apartment in Ottawa, and the work would clearly be meaningful; after consulting Beth, I said yes.

And yet despite the work I was accomplishing, the anguish that led me to that park bench remained undiminished. By day, I was one-hundred-percent engaged, giving my all to each endeavour, each person, each cause. By night, I was one-hundred-percent at the mercy of the horrors. I was riding on pure adrenalin. It was just like being in the field; I was pushing not just the positive, but *everything*, to the extreme. Each night, I battled the demons of my mind and gave in to the spirits of the genocide. And it was those spirits that pushed me—just months after the park-bench incident—into taking on my most taxing endeavour of this period: writing *Shake Hands with the Devil*, the book that detailed my experience in Rwanda.

There were lots of good reasons to take on the writing of this historical account. While the genocide was getting a lot of attention now, there was next to nothing out there about the pre-genocide period and how we had arrived at that point of madness and cruelty. This was critical information to bring to light if we were to learn anything from Rwanda that would prevent such mass atrocities in the future. Also, I wanted to write it for my children, to help them finally understand why their father came back from his mission such a different person; to give them a place where they could find the whole story as I had experienced it. Someday they would want to know, and I didn't want them to have to sift through accusations against me or false revisionist theories just to get to the truth of what their father did. As Brent Beardsley put it, "If we don't get our story down on paper, we'll have to deal with our grandchildren coming to us and saying, 'Why did you allow all those people to die?'" I did not want to engage in an exculpatory exercise: in fact, my injury guaranteed that was I was unable to do anything other than relentlessly blame myself for what had unfolded on my watch. But Brent convinced me that the aim of the book would not be to justify my actions, but to get my perspective of the events and the interactions of all the players finally on the record.

It turned out that several publishers were interested in working with me, but the one I chose was Random House Canada, whose head, Anne Collins, had published *The Lion, The Fox and the Eagle*; through her editorial work with Carol Off she was already immersed in what had happened in Rwanda. Luckily, the advance the company offered was sizeable enough that I could employ help to put the research together and get the manu-script into shape. Brent came on board to assist me in sorting through the mountains of material and provide his perspective on the events. But he still held a full-time job in the military and I needed full-time help, so I hired a bright, accomplished journalist to help me get my own recollections and reflections on paper. Sian Cansfield came highly recommended: she had travelled to Rwanda, so knew the landscape that haunted me, and she had worked as a researcher on Carol Off's book and with such respected news outlets as CBC's *the fifth estate*.

Over the course of a year, Sian recorded hundreds of hours of interviews with me, pushing me deeper into my memories than even my therapists had. The horrors I'd witnessed, the abject abandonment of a people, my inner torment: it all spilled out of me into her tape recorder and her open, empathetic mind.

She became so devoted to the project that she moved from Toronto to a hotel in Ottawa, and eventually into my living room in Gatineau. She picked up my rhythm of work and made it her own, working day and night, catching a few hours of sleep on the sofa. When too many demands on my time distracted us from our work in Gatineau, I decided to retreat to Quebec City to hide away and write, and she came with me. Beth bore the invasion with the same sangfroid she did all my work, though I know she did not like the thought of me once more being so consumed by the genocide. And it wasn't long before I realized that inflicting this writing process on my family was untenable, and we moved the project back to the apartment in Gatineau.

Warm and affectionate as well as brilliant, Sian was completely devoted to the book at the same time as always caring about the impact of it on me. She'd had experience with telling difficult, even traumatic, stories. She had investigated abuse and scandal in the federal women's prison system for Louise Arbour, and was at this time also embroiled in a top-secret investigation of illegal weapons smuggling for a major news outlet. But as it turned out, she was unexpectedly fragile.

Our publication deadline was the fall of 2002, and we were meant to start delivering chapters by January of that year. Though we already had a couple of thousand pages of material, we hadn't yet begun to recount the events of 1994 from April 6 onward: the actual genocide. Anne was anxious about the material we were producing. In late spring she came to Ottawa to spend three days with us to help get us on track, and by the end of those days we had the preface and most of Chapter 1; she was certain we'd have to postpone the book a season at least, maybe longer, but Sian told her she really wanted to try to crash it out, and Anne was willing to give us a chance.

But after Anne left, the work once again stagnated. Sian never said or did anything that indicated how badly she was struggling—not to me, and not to Anne who checked in with her by phone every workday—but by the end of May I thought that if we were going to get it done, Sian needed a break. She had taken so little time off, and was so deep in the content, I thought the best thing was to extract her from it, give her time to catch her breath. And so, as I had often done with staff in Rwanda who were feeling overwhelmed, I told her to take some R & R—four or five days with her friends in Toronto—so she could come back to the project with fresh eyes.

In the early morning of Saturday, June 1, 2002, the telephone rang in my apartment in Gatineau. I was in bed, asleep, and Brent was crashed on a cot in the living room. Neither of us answered the phone. If only we had.

I ache to write these words.

When we woke around seven o'clock, I checked the messages and heard Sian apologizing, saying we were better off without her, saying goodbye. There was traffic noise in the background.

I immediately called the Toronto police and, as calmly as I could when every muscle in my body was trembling, asked the officer who answered, "Have you received any information about a potential suicide this morning?"

After questioning me, the officer confirmed that a woman meeting Sian's description had leapt off the Bloor Street viaduct into the Don River. I stood in disbelief, paralyzed at what I had just heard.

I flew to Winnipeg for Sian's funeral. Before the official visitation, I sat alone by the coffin for hours. I could not believe that I had missed that she was suffering, had not seen that she was on the verge of suicide. I cried so hard and so long. I cried for Sian, I cried for the comfort and support she had given me at the expense of her own needs, and I cried because it felt to me that Rwanda was *still* killing people. My friend, my colleague, another victim of the genocide.

Despite my anguish over Sian's death, Anne and Brent pressed me not to give up on the book, and likely saved me from myself in doing so. But I could not allow another person into the loop, couldn't risk another loss like the loss of Sian. First, Anne postponed the book a full year. She gave me the summer off to try to regroup, and then in September she and Brent stepped into Sian's role.

Over the next year, they were with me, step by step, sentence by sentence, finishing the work that Sian and I had started. It wasn't easy: at one point, I moved to Toronto so I could go to the Random House offices every day to work. I don't know what her colleagues thought when I had to get up and pace the halls with Anne as we hashed out how to express some difficult aspect of the account, weighed how much of the reality of the genocide a reader could be expected to bear. I was also forced to confront more evidence of what PTSD had done to me.

As Anne returned each chapter to me for a final review, I found myself unable let it go, to accept that the account was finished. I was sure we had left vitally important things out, that we hadn't captured all the threads. I would start rewriting, putting in everything I thought we'd missed, blowing up each chapter to three times its size. Then Anne, after reassuring me that what I thought was missing was actually there, that a reader would get it, would have to cut it down again. Still, I couldn't accept her judgement that we were covering everything I considered crucial.

The last straw was a stress-related loss of vision in one of my eyes, which made reading near impossible. For the final fact-check and review, Anne came to Ottawa for a week, and read every chapter out loud to Brent and me, entering the last round of corrections and changes on her laptop. She had hit on the idea that a general who has had to process multiple, oral reports from the field might be better able to keep the complex threads of his own story straight if he heard it, rather than read it: it turned out she was right.

In October 2003, *Shake Hands with the Devil: The Failure of Humanity in Rwanda* was in bookstores, and a year later it was in the hands of practically every person in the courtroom at the International Criminal Tribunal for Rwanda. Nothing about the writing of the book had been cathartic, as people often assumed it must have been. Getting it all down on paper had not provided any relief. But at least when I saw my account, so heavily researched, so hard won, in that courtroom, I felt I had successfully completed at least one mission.

The challenge of Arusha was more difficult this time than before. In 1998, my testimony had served to contextualize the genocide and provide a fuller picture of what had happened. Now, in 2004, the court had finally brought three Rwandan military commanders to trial on charges of genocide, war crimes and crimes against humanity. The prosecution had asked me to take the stand to help put these bastards away. I needed to go into even more detail than I already had about every interaction I had had with each of the three accused. And my testimony was critical to their prosecution, since I was the only person from the international community who had had regular contact with them before and during the genocide.

The defence was attempting to prove there had been no geno-cide, but rather a free-for-all on both sides: a natural consequence of civil war. The defendants' lawyers picked apart every word I said on the stand, and each night my team of civilian and mil-itary lawyers, Harvey Yarosky and Lt.-Col. Ken Watkins, along with a research assistant, Françine Allard, would go over the day's testimony with me and prepare me for the next. Luckily, the Department of National Defence had sent a psychiatrist along who stayed with me the whole time.

Also with me the whole time, sitting on the other side of the fluorescent-lit courtroom, was Théoneste Bagosora, the Hutu extremist who had been the Rwandan minister of defence's chief of staff and one of the main organizers of the slaughter. That was the real challenge; I had not been so close to him since the height of the genocide. I struggled with the desire to pull out a gun and blow his head off. Luckily, I wasn't armed—though there was a fully armed joint task force commando between me and the benches of the accused as a security measure. When they brought Bagosora to the witness box in handcuffs, I locked my eyes on him, though he kept his face averted and never once looked up at me. I felt launched back in space and in time to the days of the genocide; just him and me, again.

I sat, listening to his lawyer's revisionist interpretations, and thought that if Bagosora had had any honour at all, he would not have allowed such grotesque lies to be told, even in his own defence. A wordless hatred boiled inside of me and I clamped it down, with my jaw locked and my hands clenched.

I was so transfixed I did not realize that the testimony was over until I felt a gentle pat on my arm. "Come on, Meo," Harvey said. "Time to go."[*]

Soon after that second trip to Arusha, I went back to Rwanda for the first time since 1994, a trip documented in the White Pine Pictures film *Shake Hands with the Devil: The Journey of Roméo Dallaire*. I had been thinking of going back even before the tenth anniversary of the genocide, but I had wanted to do it differently. Official ceremonies weren't important to me, nor did I need an anniversary in order to remember. Not a day went by that I wasn't consumed by the genocide, so there was nothing special about the tenth anniversary for me, any more than the ninth, or eighth, or seventh.

I had hoped to return and walk the hills again. To commune with everyone who had lived through it, too. I fantasized about throwing on a pair of shorts and some flip-flops and spending a year wandering the countryside. I had agreed to do the film because I understood what films can do in terms of raising awareness, but it wasn't my preferred option to go back to Kigali with an entourage and a camera in my face.

The trip proved to be less emotionally upsetting than I had feared, likely because of the artificiality of travelling with a film crew and always trying to pretend they were not there. I was constantly being asked for my reaction, my innermost thoughts, on seeing again all the familiar sites (many still in shambles ten years on: sometimes intentionally preserved that way, some still a mess because they had been abandoned); the camera forced me to be

---

[*]   All three accused were finally convicted, though it took years of hearings and appeals to do it.

stoic. And Beth had agreed to come with me. At last she could see with her own eyes the country and the people that I was so committed to.

At the main anniversary event in the Kigali stadium, I met with Tutsis who had survived the brutality of the genocide in ways I could not fathom but deeply admired. I was dismayed to discover that they had been displaced by the Tutsi diaspora who returned after the fighting stopped. Many who had stayed through the genocide had also stayed in Rwanda, rather than fleeing, through independence in 1962, and had also lived through the subsequent coups and civil wars. But they were often treated as collaborators instead of courageous survivors. They received no compensation for their losses or acknowledgement of their agonies during the genocide. If they had died, they would have been honoured and commemorated, but because they were alive they were treated with suspicion, like second-class citizens or worse. This injustice shook my feelings of commitment and faith in the Rwandans' desire for nation-building. Not only did reconciliation between the Hutus and the Tutsis remain extremely challenging, but there were clearly serious divisions within the groups, too. I was amazed that after having been taught the consequences of such discord in the bloodiest and most murderous of ways, they were still capable of maintaining divisiveness and hatred. The situation left me with a dangerous feeling of fatalism.

I was disappointed, too, by my encounters with the Belgians during this trip. Not with the father of a peacekeeper who had died under my command, who ran up and punched me in the back; I understood his visceral anger and grief. So much so that, when I learned there would be widows of some of these peacekeepers at a presentation I was to participate in, I stopped in the lobby to ask another Canadian who was present, the journalist Allan

Thompson, to find out if I could meet them. But he warned me that the presentation had started early, and that a Belgian senator who had unexpectedly taken the microphone had chosen to use this forum in front of international media to attack me personally. I barged into the room, marching right up the centre aisle to the podium. Our terrible public confrontation put me in such a rage that any attempts at reconciliation that day were impossible. Allan told me later it was like a scene out of the Wild West.

Toward the end of the trip, Beth and I and the documentary crew visited two of the pinnacles of Rwandan culture. Both had been destroyed in the genocide and were still desolate and dead.

One was a convent just north of Kigali, called St. Andre's. It had been run by Belgian nuns for generations, and had housed a church, a school and a large open yard, all beautifully situated at the top of a hill overlooking lush green plantations. When I had visited it before the genocide, the nuns had been teaching the girls fine needlepoint stitched with silk thread; they were producing such masterful pieces I could have sworn they were paintings. The nuns encouraged the girls to sing as they worked, and they sounded like angels in three-part harmony, up there on that hill, so close to heaven. For me the place had represented the spiritual strength of Rwandan society.

The other site was the art and architecture school in Ruhengeri. It had been the only such institution in Rwanda, and before the war it, too, had thrived as a beautiful place of artistic expression, filled with bright colours and dynamic, creative young people.

We visited these sites and found the classrooms still empty, the windows and doors still busted, the work long destroyed. In ten years, no one had been able to breathe life back into them. Of course, the country had come a long way in terms of rebuilding roads and restoring necessary infrastructure, but I felt that an entire cultural dimension of Rwanda had been slaughtered and remained dead. Without that, how could the Rwandan people's soul come back to life?*

On our way to the university in Butare (which, in contrast to the convent and art school, was fully functional), we stopped at Bisesero. At the start of the genocide, the Tutsi population of this town—about a hundred thousand strong—fled to the hills. Unbelievably, over the following three months they managed to resist the Rwandan government forces and militia with such determination and vigour that about twelve thousand of them survived. This feat of arms by civilians determined to defend themselves, with nothing but makeshift spears, bows and arrows, was worthy of the annals of human survival against impossible odds. They only came out of the hills when a patrol of French forces promised to evacuate them. However, instead of remaining with the people and calling for support, the French withdrew to their base to arrange transport. By the time they came back three days later, almost every last one of the Tutsis had been slaughtered.

When we reached the university, I made a speech to the student body. Compelled by what I had seen and the dread those sites had inspired in me, I articulated, strongly and clearly, my belief that self-interest had dominated the West at the time of the genocide, and *still* dominates the West. And Rwanda, I warned the students, had to build up all its resources and strength, because if there was another crisis, no one would come to its aid. Again.

---

* When I returned home from this trip, I pulled out the box of torn and broken artwork, including one of those fine needlepoint pieces, that I had bought in Rwanda and had destroyed in a drunken rage. I spent ages gluing, repairing and reframing them in an effort to bring them back to life.

It was really only then that I had to admit to myself that my ten years of talking about it and working on it had essentially done nothing to change the international situation. Rwanda had not recovered; it was still reeling from the genocide, ten years on. The country and its people still seemed terribly vulnerable. I knew what my therapists, my friends and my family would say, and did say, repeatedly: *Roméo, it is not your fault*. The voice in my head emphatically disagreed.

As a small antidote to all this sadness, when we were driving back from St. Andre's, we stopped for a few minutes on a hilltop in Kinihira. It was the spot that I had used as my place of solace and reflection during my tour of command. It remains a beautiful view, where three magnificent valleys come together, blanketed with tea plantations and carved with rivers. Higher up, above the misty clouds, are the slopes and peaks of the hills on which most Rwandans live: lush gardens and homes dot the landscape, bright garments fluttering on clotheslines.

As Beth wandered nearby, I sat on a rock and looked across the slowly shifting clouds to the horizon of volcanoes, just as I had done ten years before. A rooster was crowing, and a few cows lowing. In that peace, I was reminded of how I had wanted to return to Rwanda, confident that here I could actually, finally, mourn. Back home, nothing put me in the state of mind to mourn; quite the opposite. Yet if I could come back again, not on an official visit like this one, but on my own, and become immersed in the life of these hills, I thought, it could happen.

The saying that there is a body under every tree in Rwanda rang in my head as I sat on that rock, with the thick tropical forests spreading out below me in all directions. I felt enchanted, as if I had been promised that I could come back here and touch all those lost souls. I could walk the hills with the rain on my face and feel at peace with them. This was where I could find serenity. Here, I could find reconciliation with all of those that I had let down.

Sadly, that heightened sense of connection didn't last. Back in the car, back on the plane, and back home, the "real world" soon caught up with me again.

In the four years since I'd folded up my uniform (and even in the six years before that after my return from Rwanda), I had felt the split in my soul grow deeper. Outwardly, I was empowered by some modest successes and the potential to do good. I was building a company, Roméo Dallaire Inc., to put some structure into my exhausting speaking schedule and to better manage my money. I remained committed to injured veterans and heavily involved in fighting the bureaucracy on their behalf. I'd been invited by the director of the Harvard Kennedy School's Carr Center for Human Rights Policy, Samantha Power, to do a year-long fellowship on conflict prevention at Harvard. *Shake Hands* had found a readership beyond my expectations, and had received the Governor General's Literary Award for Non-fiction.

Yet, my internal life was still bleak. I was still roaming at night, suffering cruelly from night terrors that plagued me through the sleepless darkness and only left me at the first signs of day.

I was no longer drinking—I couldn't, because of the medications I was now taking. But the anguish that might lead again to purposeful self-destruction stayed with me. I leaned heavily on my surrogate family—Christine, who was like a twin sister who knew my mind and heart as if they were her own, and David Hyman, who had become my private secretary and was like a cultured, caring older brother, always looking out for me. They both continued to be on high alert throughout the nights I was home. And when I travelled, the hotel staff were asked to knock on the door every two hours from midnight to dawn to ensure I was okay.

I was continuing my therapy, taking my medications, and going home to see my family on weekends. But none of it was doing a damn thing to shake the pain, to ease my suffering. It seemed nothing would let me live again, or die.

O let me be awake, my God!
Or let me sleep alway.

I could not seem to destroy myself, but neither could I live.

The pang, the curse, with which they died,
Had never pass'd away:
I could not draw my eyes from theirs,
Nor turn them up to pray.

CHAPTER FIVE

Like one, that on a lonesome road
Doth walk in fear and dread,
And having once turned round walks on,
And turns no more his head;
Because he knows, a frightful fiend
Doth close behind him tread.

FOR TEN YEARS, MY injury had completely dominated my inner being. When I could not keep that injury from affecting my daily life (and, therefore, my work), it had almost destroyed me. And yet I had borne private and public demolition, and somehow survived.

Over the next ten years, things started to feel a little different to me in one important way: from the moment I got back from Rwanda, I had worked to keep the horrors of the genocide alive and had lived a *Life-in-Death*, stuck in the past. At last I found myself actually wanting to add a mission of the future, one in which I could make a positive difference. Of all the causes I had taken on over the years, one seemed the most pointedly about the future: the use of child soldiers had been one of the most insidious elements I had witnessed during the genocide, but I believed I could see ways to take it on.

My years as special adviser on war-affected children had allowed me to reflect with intensity on the children of the Interahamwe, whom I had faced daily in Rwanda. Sharpening that focus was the official visit I made in 2001 to Sierra Leone, when the war that had engulfed that country for over a decade was ebbing. There, I met with the government about child protection, discussed tactics with the UN force commander with regard to troops facing child soldiers in conflict situations, and visited several rehabilitation sites that were part of a child soldier demobilization project. I spoke with many of the boys and girls who had been rescued and taken to these sites by UNICEF, including at one site specifically set up for pregnant girls and new mothers, all victims of rape. Though gruelling, the trip had been a godsend for many reasons. For one, it showed me that there were benefits to being out of uniform: I was able to engage more closely and more meaningfully with NGOs. And yet, because I was a general, I saw things on the ground in a humanitarian mission from a unique perspective that let me understand the military stakes in armed conflict. My background made it possible for me to take a different approach with the men who were deploying child soldiers in their ugly wars. That trip also helped me think about the issue from the point of view of the child soldiers themselves.

For years I had been haunted by the total commitment I had seen in the very young men (and some girls) of the Rwandan youth militia, who showed such blind devotion to the repugnant cause that had been imposed on them by ruthless, evil adults. Meeting similar children in Sierra Leone, I recognized that, although they were victims, they were not weak. They had been developed, during their most malleable and impressionable years, into brave, skilled combatants who were capable of unimaginable brutality. Their fervour and their versatility made them an almost perfect "weapon."

This realization—that in terms of war-fighting they were an effective weapon—shocked me. So much so that by the time I was set to start my conflict studies research at the Carr Center at Harvard in the fall of 2004, I had changed tack entirely. The international community's bungling in Rwanda had not been a unique or singular event, but rather the predictable result of an outdated approach to a new kind of conflict that was flaring up more and more often in the messy post–Cold War world. I had wanted to consider innovations in thinking that could be applied not only to the violent conflicts of this new world disorder that we had stumbled into, but also to prevention of the conflicts in the first place. However, I could not forget the disquieting revelation I'd had about child soldiers. And that became the focus of my time at Harvard. My thinking culminated in a research report called *Children in Conflict: Eradicating the Child Soldier Doctrine*. By this point, I had come to view child soldiers as not only an effective weapon, but also as the most complete end-to-end weapon system in the inventory of contemporary war machines.

It may seem odd to say it, considering what I spent my time thinking about, but I loved everything about my year at Harvard. My research assistants were first class, keen to engage in developing policy frameworks for real world problems, and my mentor, Michael Ignatieff, who had become the director of the center, strongly supported my new mission and delved deeply into the issue of child soldiers with me. When I was not flying off to give speeches or fulfill other obligations that I couldn't manage to avoid, I was immersed in interesting discussions and crucial research day and night, and I found it healing. The grounds were beautiful, the buildings were steeped in history, and the atmosphere constantly reminded you that this was the birthplace of important ideas. Generations of great minds and great ideas had created a palpable energy on that campus that I found inspiring.

The time I spent thinking about child soldiers at Harvard changed my life. Over the next five years, it led me to write another book, *They Fight Like Soldiers, They Die Like Children: The Global Quest to Eradicate the Use of Child Soldiers*. I also set up my own institute to study the issue in depth and formulate practical solutions for the eradication of the use of children as weapons of war: the Roméo Dallaire Child Soldiers Initiative. Slowly, but absolutely, the cause of child soldiers became my primary mission, and one to which I eventually dedicated the rest of my life.

In the meantime, however, Paul Martin, the prime minister of Canada, presented me with another mission: an appointment to the Canadian Senate.

Starting as a senator on Parliament Hill in 2005 made me as buoyant as being at Harvard, but times ten. I felt my new role as a great responsibility, but also as an enormous privilege. And I admit I had a moment or two where I couldn't help thinking, *Look, that's me, a poor francophone boy from East End Montreal, holding one of the highest seats in the country.* By entering the parliamentary body that approves legislation and conducts studies to guide government action, I could finally make concrete and significant contributions to issues that urgently required government involvement, but had so long remained unresolved. I was thrilled as I considered the action that now, as an insider, I could press our government to undertake: operationalizing the responsibility to protect (R2P) doctrine to prevent mass atrocities and genocide; replacing the outdated and unresponsive Veterans' Charter of 1943; bringing the anti-nuclear movement to the fore; implementing the changes Canada had agreed to when we signed the International Convention on the Rights of the Child by creating a children's commissioner, and actively engaging in the fight for the cessation of child trafficking and the recruitment of children in the world's increasing civil wars. As a senator, I could initiate legislation and present my arguments to the highest authorities in the land.

When the nomination had come in, David Hyman and I had discussed these exciting potentialities. He was pleased for me, hoping that the Senate would give me structure. "You're going in all directions," he'd said. "You've got no staff, no resources. The Senate can give you focus, and the opportunity to properly accomplish your work."

Brent, too, was pleased. Shortly after I took up my post, he came to visit me in my office in Centre Block, right in the middle of it all. He was glad to see me back in the saddle.

"Ever since they took the uniform off you," he admitted to me, "I've been waiting for the call that you were dead. But now you've got a new mission, sir!"

A mission, indeed, and a full-time job again for the first time in five years. But for all my recent improvements—both internal and external—I was soon back to my old ways and old dysfunctions. My injury was as pervasive as ever.

Despite the new demands of my Senate position, I didn't cut back on the other work I had taken on. In my spare time, I was getting the Roméo Dallaire Child Soldiers Initiative off the ground and writing a book on child soldiers. I also started my own foundation for children from underprivileged backgrounds in Quebec. I sat on the United Nations Advisory Board on Genocide

Prevention, and on the board of the Montreal Institute for Genocide Prevention. I advised on a feature film about Rwanda, based on my first book.[*]

I became a patron of the Global Centre for the Responsibility to Protect, and the Pugwash Peace Exchange promoting nuclear disarmament, as well as Biathlon Canada. I took on many honorary positions with many institutions, from the National Psychiatric Association to the Quebec Parkinson's Campaign to the 6th Artillery Regiment to UNICEF Canada. I accepted honorary degrees from dozens of universities all over the world. I realize I could have said no to the latter; many do, feeling they take up time and provide little but bragging rights. But I accepted these degrees not for reasons of ego or status, but because each occasion afforded me the opportunity to speak to new graduates and future leaders. My years of talks to community groups and private sector organizations had been informative for the public, I hope, but had yet to yield any concrete change. I thought by addressing the graduating classes from the world's best universities, I might be able to have some small impact on future leaders.

On one very typical weekend during this time, I left my office at the Senate at 1800 hours and flew to Washington, DC, to speak

---

[*]   Back in 2004, Hollywood had released *Hotel Rwanda*, a movie from the revisionist perspective of the manager of Hôtel des Mille Collines. He was portrayed as a saviour of Tutsis, whereas the UN force commander was portrayed as a gun-toting, overreacting, low-level officer. I had been really annoyed by how this piece of fiction had so strongly and wrongly informed the public debate about Rwanda. In 2007, a film company put out a feature film starring Quebec actor Roy Dupuis that built its script from *Shake Hands with the Devil*. As a Canadian production, it had a far smaller budget and a far smaller influence than the earlier film, but I found it to be an outstanding depiction of the events and of the ethical and moral impacts of such a mission on the commander.

at a university that night and then attend a breakfast meeting at the embassy first thing in the morning. Immediately after, I got back on a plane, stopping over in Toronto to talk with one of my research assistants, to sit for an interview on child soldiers with a journalist, and to meet briefly with my editor on my progress on the second book. After making a quick call to order the flowers I sent to my ailing mother every week, I was supposed to fly on to Ottawa to pick up my black tie and medals, and proceed in a rental car to the mess dinner of the artillery branch of the army in Shawinigan, Quebec. As a senior gunner, I was expected to attend this annual formal gathering of the officers of the three Quebec militias and the regular force regiments, and it was no burden at all. In fact, it was always a highlight of my year: a time to see old friends and mourn those who had left us, as well as recharge our batteries.

The event always went late, so I intended to stay overnight and then drive on Sunday to Quebec City to see Beth and do some work around the house, before returning to the Senate first thing Monday morning for a Senate defence committee meeting. But the plane was delayed out of Toronto, so I was pressed for time to get to the dinner (the protocol before supper is rather elaborate and very much part of the event; I did not want to disrespect these efforts by being late). I didn't have time to change my clothes, so I just got in my car and took off. It was snowing, which slowed me down even further, and I worried about when I was going to be able to change for dinner. Then I spotted a Port-a-Potty that had been set up for a road crew. It was dark and deserted, so I pulled over and used it as a handy dressing room to get into my formal wear. This sort of episode was entirely par for the course.

And so, as before, I was back to that demanding pace, never saying no, just accepting more and more work all the time, plugging every minute with work, with travel, with meetings, with writing, with speeches, with road-running back and forth to Quebec City.

I was always out, always doing things, but it was always work-related. I would attend the odd military event, but I never went to the mess informally to socialize. I never went to the movies or the theatre. In twenty years of almost constant travel, I never once went to the hotel bar or the pool, or took advantage of any recreational amenities. I travelled to some of the most beautiful places around the world for meetings or speaking engagements, but I didn't do any sightseeing, and I never attended the social hour after any official event. As soon as was possible, I would just go hide in my room.

While I smiled and joked in public, I did it to make others comfortable; I never allowed myself one iota of pleasure or relax-ation. I would humbly accept their kind words and applause, sign books and pose for photos, and then lock myself in my room to spend hours and hours bouncing off the walls, unable to sleep and unable to concentrate. I was consumed by the thought that I had duped the kind people who had just listened to me, who had applauded me, but did not know how damaged I truly was. Such were my nights, until dawn broke and I would pack for my early flight back to blessed work.

Whether this behaviour was intentional self-flagellation or clinical social anxiety, I am not sure. Either way, it was directly linked to my injury, and despite all the pills and all the therapy, despite the positive work on my plate, I could not heal and my mind refused to allow me to move on.

Worse, in my secret heart, I harshly judged friends from the past, my classmates and old colleagues, as well as family members, who didn't want to engage in the causes I felt were so urgent.

They kept telling me to slow down, that I was working myself into an early grave, but they didn't want to help me carry the burden. And anyone new I met, who might have become a friend, I put to work. It was the only way I could relate.

I involved my best friend, Paul Bourget, in a campaign to create a museum at the Collège militaire royal de Saint-Jean; whenever we spoke, I only wanted to talk about the work. While our chats were always friendly and warm, we no longer discussed art or music or poetry—the ties that bound us back when we were roommates in military college. Every year he and a group of other old friends invited me to go fishing, and every year something would come up. I never made it once. I'm sure I would have loved it—I find real solace in nature—but I never allowed myself the time, never felt I could abandon my terribly urgent work. Just like I didn't "have the time" to sit down and just talk to my children. And now dear Paul is dead—snatched from us too early by cancer—and oh how I miss him.

From the outset, my involvement in the Senate was exciting, but as I tackled the issues that related most closely to my expertise, I exacerbated my injury: child protection, aboriginal affairs, the responsibility to protect doctrine, veterans' welfare, defence policy, human rights and international affairs. I'd asked Hélène Ladouceur, who had been my secretary at the military college and also the college administrator, to set up my Senate office and be my chief of staff. Her mastery of both official languages, as well as military matters, made her an invaluable asset on all of these difficult files.

Often, when I spoke on these subjects in debate in the Red Chamber of the Senate or even in committee, I would feel my hands begin to tremble, and tears would sometimes come to my eyes. I would notice that the usual background of murmurs and shuffling papers would cease and the room would fall silent. My staff and others told me that my level of emotional engagement was creating unusual receptiveness among my Senate colleagues. I was glad for this, but it was not my intention; my emotion came from the reality and the urgency of the problems, and from feeling such immense responsibility. I worried about the degree to which emotions would come over me, how overwhelmed I would often be.

As an example, I had become extensively involved in Canada's efforts to help end the refugee crisis and slaughter of innocents in the Darfur region of Sudan. During my first official visit there, I saw everything I had witnessed in Rwanda in 1994 all laid out again: a belligerent government, abuse of children as militia soldiers, abuse of women, the lack of food and the signs of starvation, foreign forces tossed into the fray by the UN and the African Union, but burdened with restrictions on their capabilities and without the proper equipment to provide even basic security.

This trip reinforced my growing interest and commitment to genocide *prevention*. At the request of Kofi Annan, who was now the United Nations' Secretary-General, I joined his UN advisory board, along with such heavy hitters as South Africa's Bishop Desmond Tutu and Australia's Gareth Evans. Together we tried to assist Annan in discerning where to put the United Nations' efforts in preventing situations from becoming catastrophic.

Up to this point I had been telling the story of a genocide, and what I'd personally witnessed. But now I felt a responsibility to take on the work of prevention in a much more deliberate way. Brent had gone on to get a master's degree in genocide prevention, and I knew I needed a better intellectual grounding, too. So I reached out to Concordia University's Montreal Institute for

Genocide Studies (MIGS). I met with the founder, Frank Chalk, and discussed with him my theories on leadership in the context of genocide prevention. I believed that we—Canada, but also all the member countries of the UN—were merely reacting to problems, instead of envisioning new ways to prevent them from occurring, and that was why we were continually responding to crises, rather than getting ahead of them.

Together, Frank and I worked over the next several years to produce a strategy document called *Mobilizing the Will to Intervene: Leadership and Action to Prevent Mass Atrocities*. The will to intervene project, as it was called, advocated for ways to practically enact R2P, the responsibility to protect doctrine (the commitment of UN member states to take action to prevent genocide and other crimes against humanity, regardless of self-interest). The will to intervene and child soldiers issues became the parallel tracks of my advocacy, guiding my work on prevention of mass atrocities, of genocide, of human rights abuses.

In the meantime, in order to educate parliamentarians and bring these issues to the attention of the Canadian government, I had also created a genocide prevention group on the Hill, encompassing all parties and all houses. I began speaking of Canada as a leading middle power with particular responsibilities in such crises: we are not a superpower; we don't aim to forge an empire; we have no colonizing past (although our treatment of indigenous peoples has taught us some very painful but important lessons); we believe strongly in human rights; and we have the tools necessary to advance those rights and make this the focus for our future.

Though this work was emotionally challenging, it was satisfying to know that as a senator I could influence Canada's response to such pressing human rights concerns. As an example, I was the prime minister's envoy to Darfur (along with Senator Mobina Jaffer and Ambassador Bob Fowler) with the aim of increasing our engagement in supporting the African Union forces already deployed in a peacekeeping role. Darfur was on the verge of going catastrophic, and I knew that my political advocacy could have a real effect in real people's lives.

That is, until a change in government thwarted all my efforts. Within days of the 2006 election, and the establishment of Stephen Harper's first minority Conservative government, I received a message loud and clear: "Thank you very much, you're excused." The Darfur file was moved to Foreign Affairs, and the government announced that Africa would no longer be a priority area for Canadian aid. The Veterans' Charter was soon watered down. Our efforts on the responsibility to protect doctrine were iced. The government pronounced Omar Khadr, the Canadian child soldier being held at Guantanamo Bay, a terrorist and denied him constitutional protection. The causes I believed in were now being blocked at every turn.

One of the first places I saw the new government's attitude clearly revealed was on the Veterans' Charter legislation I'd been helping to push. Worse, I felt implicated in the mess we made of it. As far back as my time as the assistant deputy minister (personnel) in the late nineties, I had been highly conscious of the military system's attitude on veterans, supporting the Second World War and NATO vets, but not doing much for those who had served since the end of the Cold War. Back then, a colleague and I had formed a committee to see what could change. Many of the older vets we consulted expressed their concerns that the new generation vets were dealing with much worse situations, with more complex enemies, and coming back not only to no victory parades, but not even knowing if they had accomplished anything at all. They felt these new vets were in greater—not less—need of help.

Over the years, this committee sat every few months, and moved several yardsticks to get more assistance to the soldiers and their families. Also around that time, the deputy minister of Veterans Affairs, Larry Murray, called in a professor from Western University, Peter Neary, who created an excellent, multidisciplinary advisory board to do essentially the same kind of things—grasp the system's deficiencies with regard to veterans—but with even greater rigour. Many of us got heavily involved, and I stayed on as a representative after I was released from the military.

In 2004, before I became a senator, Peter Neary and I went to Parliament to present the report we had produced with the multidisciplinary advisory board on creating a new Veterans' Charter, which spelled out the reforms that needed to happen. The "Neary Report" was good stuff, and even old guard guys got behind it. It proposed more than a charter: a covenant between the people of Canada and its veterans, providing a cradle-to-grave commitment to those who pledged themselves to protecting the country at the risk of their own lives.

Over the years we'd been working on it from the outside, a bureaucratic bunch inside Veterans Affairs Canada had also been mandated to produce a new charter. However, *their* guiding principle was to control or even reduce costs, because the department had been assuming that the old vets from the Second World War and Korean War would be dying off, and they would soon be shutting down—despite the growing evidence that we were facing an increase in veterans sorely wounded in the new complex missions.*

The charter that the bureaucrats produced was a far cry from the promise of enduring responsibility that the Neary report recommended. Instead, in my opinion, it was a truly awful, modified peacetime worker's-comp-style insurance policy that benefited the system more than the veterans and their families.

Fast forward to my first month in the Senate, when I was asked by the Liberal government to present a bill based on the bureaucrats' version in the Red Chamber. Along with Peter Neary, I had objected vehemently to this watered-down charter, but we were told it was too late to amend it, since Prime Minister Martin and the other party heads collectively wanted to present it at the sixty-fifth anniversary of the Canadian liberation of Holland and then fast-track it through the House of Commons. I was promised, however, that if I agreed to present it, we could amend it later. The minister in charge vowed that it would be a living document that we would revisit every six months to make all the necessary amendments. I was a rookie, and politically naive, so I agreed.

Six months later, the government changed. Afghanistan was huge in the news media, and veterans were top of mind. The Conservatives, anxious to address this, announced the implementation of the charter. I was delighted with their zeal, until I realized that they intended for the bill to go forward as it was,

---

* For decades, the prevalent definition of a veteran was a person who had fought in the First or Second World War or Korea. People with my experience were not regarded as veterans, but simply as peacekeepers who had been in conflict zones. Since we had not fought a "real" war, we should be able to master ourselves afterwards. This attitude had always been a huge hurdle: how could we secure veterans' services for troops not considered "veterans"?

with no changes. Our eight years of work was unacknowledged and dismissed. No one from the committee, not me, not Neary, no Liberals at all, were even invited to the announcement.

And so started an ongoing campaign of my own to make the Conservatives change their position, and transform the charter into the ethical social covenant we so desperately needed. So began years of bickering and arguing and being obstructed by the Conservative government, which was never going to budge, and which insisted that the era of a two-tier system of medical support (one for veterans and one for the general population) was over. They said they did not want to create a veterans' "dependency" on the Canadian people; in my view that very formulation was a perversion of what veterans should be entitled to, which was a thankful country they could actually depend on, prepared and willing to give them what they need to live decently. This government would provide services, yes (though making such benefits taxable, for the first time in history), but they would also make the budget cuts that were at the core of their platform.

I couldn't have disagreed more with this atmosphere of belt-tightening and penny-pinching instead of quality work and results. It became pervasive throughout Parliament Hill, even in the Senate. Each senator was allotted an annual budget to hire staff, and I used every penny and more of my own to ensure my recommendations and objections were rigorously researched. It shocked me when other senators prided themselves on frugal spending—which limited their research and analysis of the legislation being presented—and then often voted the party line. Was that what the Red Chamber was for? Was this what democracy boiled down to? My own staff would put in weeks of hard work on legislation, and senators from both sides would agree with the content we produced, but, when the time came, those affiliated with the sitting Conservative government were instructed to vote against anything a Liberal like me brought forward.

An example that struck me to the core was my foiled attempt to make a serious impact on government policy in regard to PTSD. As chair of the Senate veterans sub-committee, I proposed a major study to look into all the latest research on PTSD, and also detail exactly what we were doing about it now, plus gather evidence and expert advice on what we should be doing in the future. The goal, of course, being to reduce the risk of future casualties, both in theatre and back home.

The vice-chair of the sub-committee was a Conservative senator, also new, but very engaged and concerned. We hit it off right away, and made real headway in our work together. For months, we reviewed research and heard expert witnesses, and together we created a thorough report.

Unbelievably, on the morning of the report's last review, the vice-chair took the floor to argue for major, fundamental changes to the report's recommendations. After the fact, I was told by another Conservative senator, that when he had briefed Conservative party members and government officials prior to our presentation, he had been given direction straight from the PMO. His about-face was my most difficult experience in politics to that point. For him to shoot down a report he had helped to create was a terrible waste of money, energy, time and, worst of all, hope.

All my work over those nine years in the Senate seemed a succession of non-successes, and it was maddening. Politics sometimes operates so far from reality that such disappointments can seem abstract to the people making the decisions. But I knew, as I knew so many truths that others just read about, that our playing politics had real-life consequences. And the truth hit home yet again when a colleague of mine from Rwanda hanged himself, fourteen years after his return. His wife had nowhere to turn, no one to tell to her why her beloved husband had done such a thing. She was terribly hurt and angry; she had time and again reached out to him, to support him. For years he had turned away from her, and she had stayed by him, encouraged him, loved him; now she felt that he had abandoned her and their kids, entirely. I tried to explain to her that *he* hadn't done this to her, to their children. The injury had done it. The genocide had done it.

I hoped I could help her to understand that the person who killed himself was not her husband, not the man she loved. It was another person, a changed person. He may have had the same body and face, but inside that head was another man, one who could not live with himself or the pain directly caused by the mission. His injury had spiralled so deep, he had lost his link to all of humanity, not just his family. I cried as I assured her that the man she married would never have done that, but I am still not certain I helped her.

Often during my presentations to veterans, I spoke about PTSD, and how medication—like insulin to a diabetic—could help bring you back to life, give you a chance, at least, to get closer to what you were and to help you be there for your loved ones. I would argue that you might not be able to feel love in the same way, but medication certainly made it possible to regain closeness with your children and your spouse, to give them comfort and to gain some serenity for yourself. The medications could soothe the injured ogre you had become and help you be a functioning person.

Yet in bleaker times, such as the days after my comrade killed himself and I had tried to comfort his wife, I wondered. Who is the real me? Is this medicated person who I really want to be?

A man with a heart problem takes his pills to mitigate the risk of heart attack. But I take pills to alter my *self*. I am dependent on them because I am fearful of what I truly am, without the pills. I really believe that the wound I suffered in Rwanda is a war wound. Yet sometimes I can't help but think that if I'd lost a leg, I'd still be the man I was before I went. The wound I suffered, and the fact that it went untreated for so long, and then the pills I still take for it, have fundamentally altered my sense of self.

Some vets with PTSD have told me they refuse pills because they want to fix their *real* being. And I always tell them, *Hey, do you think you could grow back a goddamn leg? No. So use a prosthesis to minimize what you've lost, and build on that.* But what's the prosthesis for what's between our ears?

Earlier, I wrote about being two people since I came back from Rwanda: beyond the vague shape of the person I was before the injury, there is the person that is the result of the injury, and then there is the other person who takes the medication. I will never get back to the way I was "before," because the extreme experience of the genocide destroyed the links to the old me, no matter how I long to be that man.

I longed to mourn for Rwanda, and I felt now that I wanted to mourn for myself, too. For the person I had been. It was difficult to grasp that I didn't know myself, that I was going to end my days as somebody else, somebody who was not really me. Who might I have become, I wondered, if I hadn't been injured? Would I have been happier? As it was, I didn't like what was in my head.

Since the genocide, I've worn armour—some think that it's shining, others know that it is less so. But nobody gets in. If I wasn't taking my pills, I would be a horrible person—depressed and aggressive, no matter how much therapy I was undergoing.

My prostheses permit me to be reasonable, but is that an honest way to go through life or is it just creating a "me" that is workable for society?

What if I stopped taking my pills? Who would emerge? I would challenge myself, rebelliously: if the real, unmedicated me is an alcoholic, or an aggressive nasty beast, well then, so be it. Screw anyone around me who couldn't handle it.

Maybe I don't have the guts to be the real me. Maybe it is not all that honourable to be out there in the world doing all the good works people tell me I'm accomplishing. Maybe I just don't have the balls to be the man Rwanda made me.

Thank God, so far I have always been able to snap out of this kind of destructive thinking. Because, of course, if we who suffer PTSD succumbed to this thinking, we would destroy not just ourselves but the people who love us. The destruction would affect our families too deeply, pass on too great a legacy of suffering in their lives, even carrying over to the next generations. It is not to be thought of. Yet the thoughts still come: the desire for self-destruction, for an end.

Sadly, I was not alone in this thinking. Over one hideous week right before Christmas in 2013, first one young Canadian soldier took his own life, and then another. And another. And another. The effect of these suicides, which were splashed across the news day after day, each one compounding the tragedy, fuelled my anger over the government's endless stalling and posturing on veterans' welfare. For two nights straight I was so agitated I could not sleep at all, anxiety attacks forcing me to dwell on my feelings of responsibility for these deaths, unable as I had been to prevent them. All night I thought about these men, and how they had died so very alone, abandoned, without even the camaraderie of war. I felt a powerful solidarity with them, and could not get them out of my mind. My days were pressed with a renewed urgency to make the politicians and the Canadian military leadership see what we were doing to real people, real lives, by denying that these deaths were related to missions. I was distracted, frustrated, and fatigued.

Pulling onto the Hill at about eight in the morning on December 3, 2013, I stopped at a stop sign. The roadway was deserted. I pressed gently on the gas pedal, and the next thing I knew, I had driven into a pole.

I must have blacked out, or fallen asleep. I leapt out of the car to check if anyone was hurt. No one was, thank God, but the media still had a heyday. In the Senate session that followed, I begged my colleagues to forgive me for bringing such negative attention to the institution, and they were gracious in accepting my apology, but I was struck that none of them asked me why it had happened.

I was once again alone with the frightening reality of my continued, constant vulnerability. Of late I had enjoyed the odd moment of optimism, of peace, but such moments never lasted long. In the months to come, whenever I drove past that site on the Hill, I would ask myself, why had I made such a half-assed move? A little more to the right, a little more speed, and I would have finally gone down.

Over my years as a Liberal senator, my workload had increased exponentially. After the Harper government won its majority in 2011, sadly annihilating Michael Ignatieff's Liberals, Bob Rae, the interim Liberal leader, thought the only way forward for the party was to bring real focus and vision to bear, as well as depth and discipline to our thinking. And, with a depleted group of MPs in the House of Commons, he asked several senators to conduct comprehensive studies in various areas aimed at guiding the party's thinking on future platforms and policies. He asked me to do two such studies: on veterans and defence. I readily agreed, and was given three months to produce a draft. I brought together a team of experts from various disciplines, and we went at it with full force.

When the time came, I made my presentations, ending each with a slide providing a series of decisions the leader could take to guide the work ahead. For defence, I argued that we could no longer operate in the vacuum of pursuing our national interests as foreign policy, we also needed to incorporate international development work. For veterans, I proposed a direct assault on the mealy-mouthed version of the charter the Conservatives had brought in, replacing it with the long-neglected idea of a covenant.

A week later, the leader told the caucus that my presentations were the type of work he wanted from all the areas—not just defence and vets, but foreign affairs, international trade, justice, and development. He then told everybody that from now on anything related to Canada and the world was to go through Roméo. Everything.

My staff were pleased with the positive feedback, but highly stressed by yet another increase in their workload: this new directive meant they had to shoulder more than their fair share. My office became one of the busiest in the Senate. My therapists keep telling me to slow down, but how could I say no?

The following January, I was rushed to hospital with an apparent heart attack. Like before, it turned out my heart was fine, but the pace at which I was working was burning out my body. Alongside my commitments as a senator, the Roméo Dallaire Child Soldiers Initiative was starting to mature. Under the able direction of the executive director I had brought on board, Dr. Shelly Whitman, it was growing into a unique institution, focusing on training, advocacy and research, and presenting a new doctrinal framework for security sector actors in the prevention of the use of child soldiers. We were working now with many governments, NGOs, and militaries around the world, as well as NATO and the African Union. I began to toy with the idea of leaving the stress and frustration of the Senate to pursue my work on child soldiers full-time.

At this point, the Senate expenses scandal was building. Several senators were accused of claiming travel and living expenses for which they were ineligible, and the public was understandably livid. Suddenly, and for the first time in the institution's history, all senators were being held accountable for their spending. We were all to undergo a forensic audit, which meant that every scrap of paper, every receipt, every purchase, would be analyzed. I wasn't worried about my office's research spending; I was confident about our record-keeping and the good work we had produced. But office spending came out of a different pot than research, and it was this administrative side that was complicated because the Senate rules were nebulous and ambiguous. Hélène, my chief of staff, was anxious, even though she had ensured strict discipline in my office from the beginning. Whenever she or anyone on my staff was in doubt about whether an expense should be considered Senate work or independent work, we would write to the Senate ethics officer to seek his advice. We did this extensively, and he was very helpful over the years, even coming to my office sometimes to explain the minutiae of the rules. He used a number of our cases to demonstrate to other senators what they should keep an eye on.

But there was such a high volume of activity in my office, and therefore such a high use of resources, that there was always the potential for an accidental bookkeeping error. Because we were conscious of that, we had always been extraordinarily careful. If I had to get one of my prescriptions filled, for example, I went to the pharmacy over the official lunch hour so as not to do anything personal on the public dime. The fact that I also worked weekends, holidays and nights was beside the point.

My unofficial mentor at the time was Serge Joyal, a politically savvy senator with a lot of years in the Chamber under his belt; he had written an extraordinary book on the institution. We would often discuss legislative and procedural matters, as well as content, especially in the area of human rights. This wise owl of the corridors of power came to me one day as we were waiting for the Speaker to enter and commence proceedings. He spoke to me in French, in a very soft but determined fashion, about the upcoming audit. He warned me that he had heard the Conservatives were specifically aiming to embarrass Liberal senators in order to make hay come election time. He said that because of my public profile and because of the impact I was having on a number of dossiers, I was at the top of the list of targets.

So it seemed that I had enough of a high profile that they figured I'd make a big splash if they knocked me down. Articles that began to appear during this time, extolling my integrity, were well-meaning but made my staff and me uncomfortable; the more I was billed as a poster-boy for the Senate, the harder my opponents would push to find fault with me.

Some senators objected to the process, refusing to meet the auditors or give over their personal daytimers. But I'd been through similar exercises many times at National Defence and I had nothing to hide. We opened everything up. Hélène spent months preparing for the audit according to the auditors' stringent requirements, worried that even a small error in bookkeeping on her part would damage my reputation, and therefore the causes I was championing.

When the time came, my staff and I received the auditors and we walked them through it all. They asked a few questions, and came back for a few clarifications, and in a couple of weeks they returned to say that mine had been one of the most voluminous files they had reviewed, but it was one of the easiest to audit because everything had been laid out so completely, with nothing hidden. They found nothing to criticize.

I wasn't surprised. Everyone on my staff had done an excellent job, and we were all very diligent. But poor Hélène broke down. She had worked so long and hard to make sure everything was faultless, and now that it was over, she collapsed. That was when I decided I'd had enough of the Senate. I had nearly destroyed my staff, especially the one who more than anybody else had stood by me so strongly and faithfully. Between the audit and all of the extra work the Liberal leader had put on me—and therefore my staff—they were spent.

So, when my esteemed and admirable Senate colleague, Hugh Segal, resigned, I decided that I, too, would take this step. I did not want to leave the Senate, but to stay would be to stagnate further, and impose unnecessary and unfruitful stress on myself and my staff. I was confident I could affect more change outside of the Red Chamber.

In 2014, after I resigned from the Canadian Senate, I hired Hélène to run my personal office and continue to manage my scheduling. She also took over the role of my most trusted confidante, much as Christine and David had been. I was certain the work would be a breeze from now on, after all we had been through.

I was retired, and at last I would have much more time to concentrate my thinking and my efforts.

The trouble with this rosy vision was that once the word got out, all and sundry came out of the woodwork to ask for my time—an article here, a speech there—assuming I was sitting in the garden twiddling my thumbs. Within weeks my calendar was overflowing again, even though Hélène refused eighty percent of the requests that were coming in.

I knew that I had to focus and preserve my energy. My role with the Roméo Dallaire Child Soldiers Initiative—originally as chief cook and bottle washer—had been strategically clarified and limited to top-level negotiations and introductions, policy development and fundraising. Shelly and I, along with our small team, were making concrete achievements in three main areas. One, delivering tactical, prevention-oriented training to security sector actors, to promote broader security sector reform. Two, conducting world-class interdisciplinary research to build—and share—knowledge, which in turn will lead to new solutions. And three, engaging in high-level advocacy activities to create and promote the political will to end the use of children as soldiers.

Over the past ten years, I had attempted to link the issues I took on, focusing and weaving them together. The use of child soldiers, for example, we discovered to be an early warning of mass atrocities, and soldiers who faced child soldiers on the battlefield, I knew, were at extreme risk of developing PTSD. An understanding of how interrelated these issues are could help to solve them. And so, between the Dallaire Initiative and the other cause I would never abandon—the veterans—I tried my best to create a reasonable, balanced workload. I created a team of ten colleagues, all deeply invested in veterans' matters (from previous chairs of veterans' committees to high-level retirees from DND and VAC) to keep a close watch on both individual cases and institutional policy.

But the requests kept coming, the demands pressing. To my existing involvements, I added the Valcartier Family Centre Foundation, as well as my own foundation, and patronage of Wounded Warriors Canada; I accepted seats on the advisory boards of the UN Institute for Training and Research, the Cardozo Law School R2P project, the Military Mental Health Research Institute, and the Council of the Friends of Rwanda; I became an honorary member of Opérations de paix, the Michaëlle Jean Foundation, the Post-traumatic Stress Disorder Association, the Nuclear Non-proliferation and Disarmament group, the Commission canadienne d'histoire militaire, the Global Centre for the Responsibility to Protect, the Royal Canadian Artillery, the RCA Heritage Campaign, the Festival international de Musiques militaires de Québec, and on and on. All this on top of my ongoing therapy: weekly with a psychologist and bi-monthly with a psychiatrist.

I got advice from all sides: slow down, establish priorities. Well, fine and good, but who should I say no to? The Secretary-General of the United Nations? The prime minister of the UK? My regiment? My therapists? My wife?

The year of my resignation from the Senate was also the twentieth anniversary of the genocide. To acknowledge the significance of the year, I had arranged for some long-neglected recognition for my Canadian team in Rwanda: the twelve staff officers who had been with me during the genocide. Twelve brave officers, only eleven of whom were with us on this anniversary, PTSD having tragically claimed the life of one dear comrade five years earlier.

Over two decades, we had maintained a fraternal bond, and gathered together every few years to reinforce our solidarity. This year, my eleven officers and I were received and acknowledged by the governor general, the chair of the Senate, and the whole of the House of Commons. A small recognition, never before offered them, for their outstanding performance in the face of unimaginable horror.

As meaningful as that ceremonial day had been, it did nothing to quiet the memories. They resurfaced throughout the entire year, often as intense as the moment they had originally happened. Most nights I stayed up, trying to fight sleep and the ugly dreams that invaded it. I was keenly aware on each given day of what had happened on that date twenty years earlier. Especially that spring and summer, each day on the calendar would spark flashbacks and nightmares.

It had been twenty years since I led soldiers under conditions of unlimited liability and extreme risk, when the air was laden with the smell of death and heavy with screams of utter despair. Twenty years since the millions who remained were left to suffer the injustice and ignominy of refugee camps, at the mercy of a world that never cared.

Twenty years. And yet I was living it again, right here, right now. How does a mind find peace when it is constantly at war and feels that it's still in the midst of human tragedies that defy description? A mind that has seen and touched and smelled and heard this reality constantly for weeks on end, and never found any solution? I damned myself, and this life that was a constant reminder of death.

And the damning is not one-sided, nor does it end. That twentieth anniversary year elicited a reawakening of genocide deniers and revisionism. Blame, again, was heaped on me—not based on the realities of my mission and actions, but on fictions and lies claiming that I was an active participant in the slaughter.

As the British investigative journalist Linda Melvern observed: "For all the survivors of the genocide, this [revisionism] causes the greatest distress. For them, the genocide is not a distant event from twenty years ago, but a reality with which they live every day."

Rwanda will never end and I will never be free. I know there is no remedy for what I saw, what I did and did not do, during those three months of hell. There are no painkillers for the angst, the guilt, and the excruciating vividness of that time and that place. The annual ritual of reliving Rwanda in its foulest of times is the curse of the survivor.

Each night I take my pills, and try to sleep with the hope that I will not awaken again amidst the roaming souls who still wander the hills of Rwanda, asking me to join them.

CHAPTER SIX

A sadder and a wiser man,
He rose the morrow morn.

W ELL, NOW YOU KNOW how it was for me—how it *is*.
I wonder, will you now hold me in contempt, knowing
as you do how far I fell? Or will my story help you
empathize with others who hurt, or better understand your own
pain? It was not easy for me to share my vulnerabilities so can-
didly, but the dark side of living with PTSD has to come out. If
it does not, the world will continue to hear of us only when we
commit suicide.

Just as I must accept that the Rwandan genocide will never
leave me, I now accept that my injury will never heal. For me,
treatment came too late. The wound was allowed to fester too
long, to infect too deeply. I can see now—as I couldn't while I
lived it—that pretty much everything I did, or that was done to
me, over those first years after I came home from Rwanda exacerbated my condition. My story, like the Ancient Mariner's, is a

cautionary tale; I am an object lesson in how *not* to treat a returning veteran with PTSD. At the time, neither I nor my colleagues
nor my superiors knew any better. We honestly believed that
hard work and a stiff upper lip was the best strategy for anyone
coming off a difficult mission; I trusted that work would see me
through. But more than twenty years later, I still take pills and
attend therapy, I still suffer nightmares and bouts of anxiety, I still
eat too much and work too hard. I am still and always mired in
the anguish of the genocide, and heartsick over a world that still
doesn't seem to care much about its most vulnerable people.

I am fully aware, never more so than now, at the end of this
often-frightening exercise of sharing my post-Rwanda life on the
page, that my injury has undermined my health, my relationships, my stability, my way forward, my joy. Courageous soldiers
serving in today's difficult and ethically ambiguous missions can
and should be treated for PTSD at its first signs; the Forces should
anticipate the need for treatment in order to head the damage
off, not just wait until a soldier is desperate enough to seek help.
And we—meaning all of us—need to shoulder our share of the
burden and recognize the contribution made by our soldiers
when they undertake such missions on behalf of humanity. We
need to insist that they are supported when they come home.

The brain is as vital to life as any organ in the human body. To
treat an injury to the brain as less urgent, less in need of care and
compassion than other, more obvious types of injury is misguided
and ignorant. Our efforts to treat our veterans with PTSD must
be comparable to our efforts to repair damaged hearts, provide
timely kidney transplants, avoid amputations or restore eyesight.
We still have much to learn about the injury, and effective treatment will differ for each individual, but anyone who recognizes
some of the symptoms I have described in this book in themselves

or a loved one should approach their doctor, or Veterans Affairs, or an organization like Wounded Warriors for immediate advice.

Urgent treatment is not only essential to the injured veterans— many of whom still have fifty or sixty years of living ahead of them—but for their families. PTSD can ripple out to harm the people around the primary sufferer: parents, spouses and children all suffer from the consequences of the injury when it results in alcoholism, abuse, neglect or divorce. Evidence is now emerging that the teenaged children of PTSD-injured vets are themselves sometimes committing suicide.

It is essential for the injured, their families, their friends and the entire care community to understand what PTSD actually is, and how it uniquely affects today's military veterans. Only when we truly understand the injury and take action to head off and to mitigate its impact will we be able to say that we recognize the real costs of peacekeeping, peacemaking and war.

The source of my injury was not experiencing the extremes and ugliness of war, per se. It was not the result of combat, or of any one specific incident. For me, and for too many other veterans, the source of this operational stress injury is repeated assaults on our most sacred and fundamental values and beliefs. The physical ramifications can be lethal, but PTSD is also a *moral* injury that ravages our minds, our souls. The constant ethical, moral and even legal dilemmas that confronted me in the months leading up to and during the genocide pounded my mind like a judge's fierce gavel, and the verdict was always *guilty*. No matter how I tried to intervene, the slaughter and mayhem, the lies and half-truths, the racism and hatred rolled on inexorably. Every fibre of my being—my belief in fairness, goodness and right action, every value instilled in me by my parents, my community, my religion, my vocation—was under constant assault from all sides. Not only from the *génocidaires*, who were massacring hundreds of thousands, turning neighbour against neighbour, and using and abusing women, children, innocents, but also from the international community. The homicidal hatred, from which I and my force could offer little protection, was one horrifying form of evil, but no less lethal was the calculated disregard with which the international community responded. It was so clear that the powers to whom I appealed did not believe those black lives mattered. If they had, they would have intervened. Nothing had prepared me or my colleagues for a situation that pitted us and all of our fundamental values and beliefs against people playing by a totally different set of rules.

Of course, the frustrations and responsibilities of command were mine alone, but PTSD hit more than just me. It hit many of my soldiers right where it hurts, not in the gut, but in the soul, the moral centre of their being.

Today there is no more explicit example of soldiers at risk of a moral injury than those who encounter a child combatant on the battlefield. I grew up, as did many soldiers, with the ideal that childhood should be a time of innocence and play; that children should be loved and protected; that the duty of adults is to help their children grow up safe and strong. Then we go abroad to serve in a mission in a failed or failing state, and we may be forced to shoot and kill a child who is bent on shooting and killing us or the people we are protecting. To face a child in battle is a gross insult to the profession of arms; it undermines and destroys the moral purpose of any military action, undermines the soldiers themselves, even before the first shot is fired. This ethical conflict is what makes the use of child soldiers so effective—it's an assault on the soul of the opposing force, just as rape as a weapon of war is an assault on the soul of the civilian population. Both go beyond our understanding, our nature. Yet, until recently, the military had not even acknowledged that our troops face child combatants, and our Forces have yet to develop training for it.

This is the core of my mission with the Roméo Dallaire Child Soldiers Initiative, the goal of which is to eradicate the use of child soldiers. There may be some salvation in finding a solution to this problem, in keeping children from being killed and keeping our soldiers from having to face such impossible decisions.

Over the years, and especially during the time I've spent on this book, I've returned time and time again to the question, *why*? Why did I, why do *we*, offer ourselves for military service? Why do we fight in the first place, and then continue to fight this injury? Why have I never let Rwanda fade, and why do I continue to fight for veterans, for children, for human rights? Why don't we just turn our backs on the needy, as so many others do? The only answer I have been able to muster is one that I saw profoundly illustrated time and again in Rwanda: it is simply who we are.

Rwanda, May 1994

I send a patrol into a village after we receive reports that the population was slaughtered earlier this morning. It appears that there is nobody left alive. At the far end of the village the patrol stumbles upon a large ditch in a cordoned-off area. It is rape site. Inside are the horribly mutilated bodies of dozens of women and girls. As his troops approach, the platoon commander realizes that some of them are still alive, barely so, but alive.

What should he do? There is a very high percentage of HIV and AIDS infection in Rwanda, and the risk of contracting the disease in these massacre sites is also high. We do not have any medical supplies to treat the survivors, nor any means of carrying them away. Also, they are so badly abused they are unlikely to survive long.

Later, I ask each of the contingent commanders what their lieutenants would have ordered their platoons to do in that situation: would they have ordered their troops to help these people in whatever way they could—maybe offering them some water or a bit of solace—or would they have ordered them to move on, since there was no way to save them, and the slaughter was happening all over the goddamn place? For weeks, all of the troops have been walking through village after village of slaughtered people; they have seen thousands of the dead and dying by this point.

Twenty-three out of the twenty-six commanders in my mission say they would order their troops to keep on going. Commanders from three countries say they would intervene: Ghana, Holland and Canada.

This particular platoon, which has just come upon the rape site, is Canadian. When the commander turns to give the order to his troops to help the women, he is too late. His soldiers—young men just nineteen, twenty, twenty-one years old—have already broken ranks and jumped down into the ditch to provide whatever comfort they can to these women and girls in their last moments.

That is *us*. It is a reflex we have. We don't even debate it. We instinctively respond when called, and we always have. It is not the instinct of all Canadians; nor is it the instinct of Canadians exclusively. But it is something I have encountered over and over in the military and in my humanitarian work since I left the military: a very human and humane kind of people who have this sense of moral responsibility. Just by picking up and reading this book you have proved yourself to be a part of it. Please understand, I don't aim to elevate myself or any particular group by saying this. There's no special merit in it: I've come to think that to care and to want to help is simply in our character. Not all of us, not all of the time: we aren't saints. There are careerists everywhere, whose only frame of reference is their self-interest. But I have seen so many soldiers humbly set out to do whatever the mission requires, thinking only of the good they can do, not thinking about themselves at all. And when they are thwarted, they are outraged and demoralized.

It is important for the troops to understand and to feel that they do come from a caring society, and that is what they are fighting

for, what they are made of. Because it is for this reason that they
serve, and sometimes it is for this same reason that they hurt. We
who suffer from a moral injury do so because of who we are, what
we have aimed to do and what we are made of. We don't shy away
from the terrible realities that our fellow humans face. And so we
are left sadder and wiser.

Because our veterans do not shy away, because they carry the
moral norms of our society into immoral situations and then
suffer the consequences, we all have a shared responsibility to
care for them when they come home. They have performed a
duty for the nation and the world, and we all must acknowledge,
not deny, what they have had to experience on our behalf, and on
behalf of all humans. Presently, we cast PTSD as an individual's
problem, but it is not, and it *must be shared.* The Ancient Greeks
made it a communal experience through the medium of tragedy,
revealing the patterns of war and the realities of the war-wounded
in such a way that personal guilt and suffering became a shared
experience.* An individual veteran's tragedy remains a tragedy,
whereas a shared tragedy can become part of a positive, instruc-
tive narrative of our country.

This brings me to the covenant I believe we owe our soldiers.
Not everyone is cut out for the work of a soldier. Not everyone
feels the moral responsibility to put their life on the line for
others. But those who do, who offer themselves to protect the
innocents of the world and then come home morally injured,
deserve more than our thanks, and the boot, and a cheque once
a month (if they're lucky).

---

* As I learned in *The Theater of War,* the book that director Bryan Doerries
  wrote about performing readings of Greek tragedies for military audiences.

If, like me, you believe that thriving nations like ours have an obligation to support efforts to build international peace and security, and to help those who are the victims of war and conflict around the world, then you must accept that we have an obligation to provide for our veterans who go out into that world and put their own lives and well-being at risk to achieve those ends.

The situation has improved in recent years, in some cases due to a genuine concern by some political leaders, bureaucrats and senior military officers, but much still needs to be done as we attempt to deal with the overwhelming number of casualties from our post–Cold War missions. We have lost more veterans to suicide during and since our mission in Afghanistan than we did in our thirteen years of combat there.

Today, the government and you and I, all of us, have a shared responsibility to heal our veterans, bring them back into the fold, and care for them for the rest of their lives. This was easier for people to understand in the days of the Greatest Generation, when the scale of the conflict meant that entire societies shared their soldiers' defeats and victories, celebrated their efforts and supported them and their families until the very end.

Now we send our troops into small, ugly conflicts in far-off parts of the world, where they face warlords and rebels and unjust regimes battling their own people, abusing their most vulnerable, and when our soldiers come back, we don't really want to hear about what they've encountered. Then we act surprised when they commit suicide. It is for this reason that I believe that we must begin to count suicides among our war dead. I believe this most strongly, because it is to those who suffer so greatly from postings to today's morally challenging missions that we owe the most, not the least.

People who join the military are often thrown into circumstances beyond their comprehension, and are ordered to try and bring an element of justice to the chaos they find there. Yet often there doesn't seem to be a hope in hell of achieving that objective. More often than not they have to leave before the job is even finished. They come back home, but now they perceive home not as the true reality but as a weird bubble of safety, a privileged place untouched by the chaos others endure. Veterans can have a terrible time reconciling themselves to that inequity.

Our veterans (of the military, but also of all the first-responder professions: police, firefighters and medical personnel) have committed themselves to a higher calling, and we need to recognize their commitment in a manner that is worthy of its importance. I believe that what is needed is a cradle-to-grave covenant that assures protection and healing not only to the physically injured but also to those morally injured in the line of duty. I propose a continuum of care that will help them to reconcile their current lives with the terrible experiences that created their injury, and allow them to rejoin society with confidence and serenity. I propose the ongoing availability of a range of supports and resources: medical treatment, of course, but also long-term therapy and later, retirement homes that specifically cater to military veterans, where they will be treated as veterans, not just patients, and will stay associated with their regiments and their traditions. I recently visited a Veterans Affairs office that had a reinforced glass partition between the veteran and the clerk; it was like a seedy pawn shop. It struck me as a real symbol of the barriers placed between injured veterans and the rest of us, even those who are supposedly there to help them. This cannot be. We must treat our veterans as soldiers throughout their lives, and give them and their families the care they need for the rest of their lives.

As I approach the end of this book, I'm also approaching my seventieth birthday. I am surprised to find that I am angry at that number—angry that I might be running out of time. For the first time since I returned from Rwanda, I am surprised to realize that my wish to end my life has been trumped by a desire to stay alive and continue my mission. I'm angry I don't have *more* time to keep working on behalf of child soldiers, on behalf of veterans, on PTSD. As I race around the globe, meeting with heads of state and international organizations—Ethiopia, Kenya, Tanzania, Uganda, Jordan, Iraq and the Hague this month alone—I'm angry that I can't do more. And I understand that the anger comes from a place of hope.

I want to be around to see the outcome of my work with child soldiers. The Roméo Dallaire Child Soldier Initiative has come so far already, and is now working in over sixty countries on advocacy and research, but also on providing tactical, field-focused, prevention-oriented training for soldiers, police officers, and other security-sector actors around the world who may encounter child soldiers—*before* they deploy.

We have begun to hire Canadian veterans, especially wounded warriors, as our international trainers in this work. Who better than a veteran of the Canadian military or police forces—with their experience, ethos and credibility—to train other soldiers and police officers? It is my hope that this project will give our veterans, so many of whom come home unfulfilled, an opportunity to return to the field and complete their mission. And these veterans may gain some measure of vindication in the knowledge that their sacrifices and experience are valuable in training others, providing them with ways to handle situations that involve child soldiers and options beyond the use of lethal force against children. In this way our veterans will regain pride in who they are.

My mission in Rwanda and my subsequent PTSD gave me insight into the problems and also the potential solutions. I have seen this in my work, when I have used my unique access to the military and humanitarian worlds to personally negotiate the release of child soldiers. And I have seen it in my personal life: for years, my PTSD kept me apart from my family. But recently my understanding of this injury, my living with it so long, has allowed us a rapprochement.

Because of what my injury put us all through, my wife is now a UNICEF ambassador and a respected advocate of family support centres. Each of my children has taken on work in the military and on humanitarian projects around the world. The insight I have gained has allowed me to reach out and offer help to my eldest son, who came home from his latest mission hurting. It has drawn us together in a deeper way than I had ever dared hope for.

This is why I have dedicated this book to my wife and my three children, and to their children: as an example to other veterans that no matter the depth of the injury, all may not be lost. Out of the darkness of my PTSD has come the capacity to understand human suffering, and with it, the first small healing rays of love.

This seraph-band, each waved his hand:
It was a heavenly sight!
They stood as signals to the land
Each one a lovely light.

ACKNOWLEDGEMENTS

I am grateful for the support and assistance of so many people in the making of this book. My warmest appreciation goes out to my core team of writers, readers, and memory-keepers: Anne Collins, Brent Beardsley and Jessica Humphreys, as well as Françine Allard, Maurice Baril, Serge Bernier, Ralph Coleman, Joe Culligan, Michael Enright, Matthew Friedman, Stéphane Grenier, David Hyman, Hélène Ladouceur, Phil Lancaster, John Lemieux, Stephen Lewis, Paul Martin, Rick McLelland, Don McNeil, Christine Morel, Larry Murray, Jean Pelletier, Jerry Pitzul, Patrick Reid, Iqbal Riza, Tom Stafford, Allan Thompson and Harvey Yarosky. Thanks also to Mike Ausdal, Richard Barrette, Jean Boyle, Frank Chalk, Robin Gagnon, Michael Ignatieff, Gord O'Conner, Carol Off, Alan Okros, Greg Passey, Landon Pearson, David Plett, Hugh Segal, Joe Sharpe and Ken Watkins.

ROMÉO DALLAIRE is a retired lieutenant-general, retired Canadian senator and celebrated humanitarian. In 1993, Dallaire was appointed force commander for UNAMIR, where he bore witness to the Rwandan genocide. His Governor General's Literary Award–winning book, *Shake Hands with the Devil*, exposed the failures of the international community to stop that genocide. It has been turned into an Emmy Award–winning documentary as well as a feature film; it has also been entered into evidence in war crimes tribunals trying the perpetrators of the Rwandan genocide. Dallaire has received numerous honours and awards, including Officer of the Order of Canada in 2002 and the United Nations Association in Canada's Pearson Peace Medal in 2005. His second book, *They Fight Like Soldiers, They Die Like Children*, was also a national bestseller. Since his retirement, he has become an outspoken advocate for human rights, mental health and war-affected children. He founded the Roméo Dallaire Child Soldiers Initiative, an organization committed to progressively ending the use of child soldiers worldwide through a security sector approach.

JESSICA DEE HUMPHREYS is co-author of the acclaimed bestsellers *Child Soldier: When Boys and Girls Are Used in War* and *They Fight Like Soldiers, They Die Like Children*.